Mission: Easter

Youth Programs & Ideas for Lent

Todd Outcalt

Abingdon Press
Nashville

Copyright © 2005 by Abingdon Press.

All rights reserved.

With the exception of those items so noted, no part of this work may be reproduced or transmitted in any form or by any means, electronic or mechanical, including photocopying and recording, or by any information storage or retrieval system, except as may be expressly permitted by the 1976 Copyright Act or in writing from the publisher. Requests for permission should be addressed to Abingdon Press, 201 Eighth Avenue, South, P.O. Box 801, Nashville, TN 37202-0801.

This book is printed on acid-free, recycled paper.

Unless otherwise noted, Scripture quotations are from the *New Revised Standard Version of the Bible,* copyright © 1989, Division of Christian Education of the National Council of the Churches of Christ in the United States of America. Used by permission. All rights reserved.

At the time of publication, all website addresses were correct and operational.

Cover design: Keely Moore.

Cover photo: "The Last Supper," by Sadao Watanabe. Used by permission of The Upper Room Chapel and Museum, Nashville, Tennessee.

05 06 07 08 09 10 11 12 13 14—10 9 8 7 6 5 4 3 2 1

Contents

How to Use MISSION: EASTER 4

Make Lent More Than a Bit of Fluff 6

Programs

Repentance: Ash Wednesday 8

Temptation: The First Sunday in Lent 10

Following Jesus: The Second Sunday in Lent 16

Faithfulness: The Third Sunday in Lent 22

Calling: The Fourth Sunday in Lent 28

Devotion: The Fifth Sunday in Lent 34

Sacrifice: Palm Sunday 40

Service: Maundy Thursday 46

Fear: Good Friday 48

Hope: Easter Sunday 50

Reproducible Pages 55

Ideas

Lenten Dramas 65

Worship Ideas 71

Lenten Retreat Plan 73

Additional Resources for Lent 74

Extra

Bible Dictionary 75

How to Use

How to Use Mission: Easter

About Mission: Easter

Lent is a season of preparation. For six-and-a-half weeks in the late winter and early spring, Christians around the world prepare for Easter, the day we celebrate Jesus' glorious Resurrection. Lent prepares you for Easter; but what prepares you for Lent? How can you make Lent meaningful for your youth?

The purpose of MISSION: EASTER is to provide youth leaders, Christian education directors, and Sunday school teachers with programs and ideas they can use in a variety of settings throughout the Lenten season. This resource will help you prepare lessons and activities that will teach youth to better understand and observe this sacred time of year.

Programs

Sunday Programs:
MISSION: EASTER contains seven programs, one for each Sunday in Lent. You can use these programs during the Sunday school hour or as a part of Sunday- or Wednesday-evening youth fellowship.

Each program is based on a New and Old Testament Scripture (from *The Revised Common Lectionary*) and a key question, which is printed in the center of the opening page of each program. Every Sunday program includes six activities related to that program's Scriptures and key question.

Each Sunday program includes a one-page article explaining how that Sunday's topic relates to youth and to the Lenten season and an easy-to-use chart that tells you the supplies needed for each activity.

Reproducible Pages: At least one reproducible worksheet supplements each Sunday program. These worksheets, some of which include prayers and readings, allow youth to express themselves through writing and roleplaying. Permission is granted to make copies of these pages for any person studying MISSION: EASTER.

Weekday Programs: In addition to the seven Sunday programs are three short programs designed for the sacred weekdays of Lent: Ash Wednesday, Maundy Thursday (or Holy Thursday), and Good Friday. These mini-programs provide devotional experiences that will give your youth an opportunity to reflect on the meaning of these important days. For some youth and possibly for yourself, these devotions will provide a much needed break from a hectic school or work week.

Bible Studies: At the end of each Sunday program is a Bible study that will give your youth an in-depth look at the week's Scripture lesson. These studies are great for Sunday school lessons or midweek Bible studies and can help engage older youth. Each Bible study encourages youth to make connections between the week's Scripture and their daily lives. The Bible Dictionary on pages 75–80 will aid the groups using these studies, though having further biblical reference materials on hand is recommended.

Lenten Dramas

Drama has a tendency to invoke emotion in ways that activities, discussions, and Bible studies cannot. Therefore, MISSION: EASTER includes two easy-to-perform skits for the Lenten season. Both original dramas, written specifically for MISSION: EASTER, are by Beth Miller, author of *Worship Feast Dramas: 15 Sketches for Youth Group, Worship, & More* and founding director of Ann Arbor, Michigan's Strangely Warmed Players. These skits can be sight-read and used as discussion starters or thoroughly rehearsed and performed in front of a congregation.

Worship Ideas

Worship, an important part of any season, fosters communal unity and individual nourishment of the spirit. MISSION: EASTER provides you with a variety of worship ideas that are perfect for Lent. From foot washing to hosting an agape feast, these ideas will help you create Lenten worship experiences that engage youths' senses and build community.

Lenten Retreat

Retreats can be spiritually refreshing at any time of year, but they especially fit Lent. The Lenten season is a time to reflect on one's life, evaluate one's spiritual health, and prepare to meet the risen Christ. Incorporating many of the programs and ideas in this book, the MISSION: EASTER retreat plan gives youth opportunities for personal and communal reflection, evaluation, and preparation.

Additional Resources

Though MISSION: EASTER gives youth leaders and Sunday school teachers plenty to do throughout Lent, no one book can cover everything. To fill in the gaps, MISSION: EASTER provides a list of resources that can supplement your Lenten programming.

Bible Dictionary

The six-page Bible Dictionary might better be described as a Bible glossary, because chances are that no Bible dictionary sitting on your bookshelf or in your church library contains only six pages.

But the Bible Dictionary provides more than just definitions. Each entry gives the user pertinent historical, geographical, and theological information as well as relevant Scripture references.

The Bible Dictionary is designed to be used with the Bible Studies at the end of each Sunday program, though you can use it to enhance several activities in this book. Permission is granted to make copies of the Bible Dictionary for any person studying MISSION: EASTER.

Lenten Advice

Make Lent More Than a Bit of Fluff

By Jeff Rasche

Growing up in the church, many of us have at one time wondered why the pastor spends six weeks in the late winter and early spring talking about the fluffy stuff you find clinging to clothes. Eventually, our parents and Sunday school teachers have explained to us that Lent is a season, an important part of the Christian calendar. But for many youth the significance of Lent has not changed much since that childhood confusion with lint. The forty-day Lenten season is just the "fluffy stuff" clinging to Easter, fluff that will inevitably be brushed off when Easter morning rolls around. As a Sunday school teacher, how can you make Lent more than just a bit of fluff?

What Is Lent Anyway?

Lent (walking with Jesus toward his sacrificial death in Jerusalem) and Advent (preparing for Jesus' birth) are two of the six seasons of the Christian year and are considered seasons of preparation. One prepares us for Jesus' birth, the other for Jesus' death. Purple, the color of both royalty and penitence, represents both seasons: During Advent we celebrate the coming of the King; during Lent we repent because of the sacrifice he made on our behalf.

Yet while Advent is marked by the hanging of the greens, the Advent candles, and a barrage of festive and familiar songs (not to mention a full-scale marketing blitz), Lent has been reduced to "that time when people give up eating or doing something." Sure, some restaurants recognize Lent with Friday fish specials; and some churches celebrate the season with a special Bible study or a series of breakfasts. But by and large Lent is not the big deal it should be.

The Lenten season is that time of the Christian year that remembers the second phase of Jesus' ministry. In the first phase, beginning with his baptism, Jesus fully devoted himself to his work as a teacher, healer, and miracle worker. After the Transfiguration, Jesus' ministry took a new direction, as he set his face toward Jerusalem and the culmination of his earthly mission. He knew that traveling with his disciples to Jerusalem for that year's Passover festival would cost him his life. Even before the Transfiguration, Jesus had told his disciples that he "must go to Jerusalem and undergo great suffering" (Matthew 16:21). As one of Jesus' closest friends, Peter would hear nothing of the sort. Yet Jesus knew that his mission was bigger than physical pain or earthly mortality. He knew that he must extend his ministry into the volatile political climate of Roman-occupied Jerusalem, even if doing so meant confronting the religious authorities. As we know, the trip cost Jesus his life, a life he gave for our sins.

In stark contrast to Easter, Lent is the "dark purple" of death and confrontation before the "victorious white" of Easter. Lent is the walk through the valley of the shadow of suffering and death. Since most of us like to avoid such painful topics, one can understand why big crowds arrive at church just in time to celebrate the last-second shot for victory on Easter morning, even though many have missed the rest of the game when "our team" looked as if it would be soundly defeated.

Mission: Easter—Youth Programs & Ideas for Lent

How Do I Make Lent Relevant for Youth?

The challenge for anyone who works with youth is figuring out how to "resurrect" the importance of the Lenten season. Here are some practical suggestions for making Lent a season to remember, not just a bit of fluff:

✝ Pay attention to your setting. Use the purple of the season, and explain its significance. Add new decorations such as thorns, nails, torn garments, and crosses that represent Jesus' suffering. Change the décor so that students notice that Lent is a special season and not just "ordinary time."

For Easter Sunday, replace these signs of suffering and death with white fabric drapery, flowers, extra lighting, flashy and colorful bulletin boards, and other joyous decorations. Make it your goal to make your youth exclaim, "Wow!" when they walk through the door on Easter. (The contrast in your room décor should suggest the sharp contrast between death and resurrection. If we don't walk through the "valley of the shadow of death" during Lent, Easter loses much of its punch.)

✝ Take advantage of the changes in nature. Natural contrasts between winter and spring as well as the radical transformations of some species parallel the contrast between death and new life. Depending on your location, you may be able to observe the transition from winter to spring. Keep track of flowers as they bloom, trees as they bear new leaves, and animals as they emerge from hibernation or return from migration. Make notes of these changes throughout the Lenten season.

✝ Do a mission project. No better season to serve people exists other than Lent. You might arrange a weekly group visit to a nursing home so that students will get to know the residents over several weeks. Consider working in a soup kitchen or on a Habitat for Humanity house on Saturdays. Through such missions, you and your youth can deliver the message that God can overcome suffering with new life and new hope. You can make this message real in the lives of people who are hurting or without hope in your community.

✝ Reach out to inactive youth. Your church probably has some families who are inactive in your congregation but come to church on Easter. This year, try to give those families or at least the youth in those families a head start. Take on a special project for the Lent and Easter seasons such as painting a mural in your meeting space or doing a weekday Bible study. Go out of your way to invite the youth whom you see only a few times a year. Even if many of these youth do not respond, the invitation itself witnesses to something important and special happening at the church. The seed you sow may grow later.

When we make Lent more than just a bit of fluff, the new life of Easter leaps out in contrast like a butterfly emerging from a chrysalis, like the "wow" of a dark room vividly lit up, and like the smile on a hungry woman's face when someone serves her a delicious bowl of hot soup.

Jeff Rasche serves two United Methodist congregations in Camp Point, Illinois. He regularly writes adult devotionals and youth curriculum, including the 2004 vacation Bible school program Faith League. *He and his wife, Shelley, have three sons: Ben, Zac, and Nicholas.*

Ash Wednesday

Repentance: Ash Wednesday

Key Verse: "For where your treasure is, there will your heart be also" (**Matthew 6:21**).

Old Testament: **Joel 2:1-2, 12-17** (Return to God, who is gracious and merciful.)

New Testament: **Matthew 6:1-6, 16-21** ("Beware of practicing your piety before others.")

Understanding Ash Wednesday

Ash Wednesday marks the beginning of Lent, the forty days (excluding Sundays) leading up to Easter. For centuries, Christians have gathered to begin Lent with acts and prayers of repentance. Christians have symbolized their commitment to repentance with an ash mark or sign of the cross placed upon the forehead or hand. This sign reminds Christian disciples to reject sin, seek God's forgiveness, and witness to others (since many people will ask about the ashes on our foreheads). So that people can wear the ashes all day, Ash Wednesday services are best done in the morning. Churches often save the fronds of palm leaves from one year's Palm Sunday celebration and burn them into ashes for the next year's Ash Wednesday service.

The Imposition of Ashes

Talk with a member of your pastoral staff about providing ashes for the occasion, or check out *www.Cokesbury.com* for a ten- or fifty-gram package of palm leaf ashes.

To conduct the ritual, stand at the front of your meeting space and instruct the youth to form a line. (If you have a large group, ask some youth or adult volunteers to assist you.) Invite the teens to come forward one at a time. If a youth would prefer ashes on the hand instead of on the forehead, have the teen raise a hand to eye level.

As you smudge the ashes on a youth's forehead or hand, say one of the following statements:

✝ Remember that you are dust, and to dust you shall return.*
✝ Repent, and believe the gospel.*

> **How do youth live as disciples of Jesus Christ?**

An Ash Wednesday Prayer †

O God,
   maker of everything and judge
    of all that you have made,
    from the dust of the earth you have
     formed us
    and from the dust of death you
     would raise us up.
    By the redemptive power of the cross,
    create in us clean hearts
  and put within us a new spirit,
that we may repent of our sins
  and lead lives worthy of your calling;
through Jesus Christ our Lord. **Amen.**

Create a Worship Experience

Use the suggestions on page 9 to create an Ash Wednesday worship experience for your youth.

* From *The United Methodist Book of Worship*, page 323. Copyright © 1992 by The United Methodist Publishing House.

† Reprinted from *The United Methodist Hymnal*, no. 353. Copyright © 1989 by The United Methodist Publishing House. Used by permission.

Mission: Easter—Youth Programs & Ideas for Lent

The Invitation

Say: "I invite you to observe a holy Lent: by self-examination and repentance; by prayer, fasting, and self-denial; and by reading and meditating on God's Holy Word. Let us make a right beginning of repentance and take note of our mortal nature by kneeling before God, our Creator and Redeemer."*

Then invite the youth to read aloud one or more of the following Scriptures:

- **Psalm 38** (This is a psalm asking God for healing and forgiveness.)
- **Daniel 9:3-5** (Daniel offers a prayer of confession.)
- **Joel 2:1-2, 12-17** (Return to God, who is gracious and merciful.)

Receiving the Ashes

Say the Ash Wednesday prayer (page 8) or another prayer that deals with repentance, redemption, and our being created from the dust of the earth. If you create your own prayer, write it on a markerboard or large sheet of paper or put it on a PowerPoint® slide.

Following the prayer, invite the youth to come forward and receive the ashes. Use The Imposition of Ashes from page 8 as a guide. For this time or worship, consider having a prayer station in your meeting space—perhaps a place for kneeling, a place for sitting and silently meditating, or a table on which you have placed images of Jesus and other Christian symbols. Also, consider singing appropriate hymns as the ashes are received. If you have access to a piano or organ and one or more of your group members play, have these youth provide accompaniment. (See the suggested hymns in the margin.)

A Gospel Reflection

Invite a youth to read aloud **Matthew 6:1-6, 16-21**. Then ask the teens to reflect on or briefly discuss the following questions:

✝ What does Jesus tell us here about praying, fasting, and giving to the poor? How well do you follow his instructions?

✝ When do you spend too much time and money on storing up earthly treasures?

✝ How can we go about storing up treasures in heaven?

✝ How might our world benefit from everyone following Jesus' advice?

✝ How can our group or congregation ensure that our motives are well-intentioned and that we are storing up treasures in heaven?

Close by singing one or more verses of "Amazing Grace."

---

* Adapted from Invitation to the Observance of Lenten Discipline, *The Book of Common Prayer*, pages 264–269. Copyright © 1979 by Doubleday.

Suggested Hymns
- "Come, Sinners, to the Gospel Feast"
- "Spirit Song"
- "It's Me, It's Me, O Lord (Standing in the Need of Prayer)"
- "Jesus, Remember Me" (No. 7 in *Worship Feast Taizé Songbook;* see page 74 for more information)

Repentance: Ash Wednesday

First Sunday

Temptation: The First Sunday in Lent

Key Verse: "For we do not have a high priest who is unable to sympathize with our weaknesses, but we have one who in every respect has been tested as we are, yet without sin" (**Hebrews 4:15**).

Old Testament: Genesis 2:15-17; 3:1-7 (Adam and Eve give in to temptation.)

New Testament: Luke 4:1-13 (Jesus is tempted in the wilderness.)

Youth and Temptation

Temptation comes in many forms, such as the lures of giving in to peer pressure, of trying destructive and addictive behaviors, and of turning away from persons in need. The Lenten season—these forty-seven days of soul-searching and journeying with Jesus toward the cross and the Resurrection—has traditionally been a time for Christians to make themselves aware of these temptations, turn away from sin, and deepen their faith in God.

Youth in particular may need some help in understanding how temptation can affect their minds, attitudes, and choices. Because temptation is often subtle (such as the urge to covet an article of clothing on a TV commercial) and alluring (such as the urge to illegally download thousands of songs for free), youth need to be aware of how the power of temptation works in their lives and in their world. Some temptations—such as the lust for revenge, sexual promiscuity, drugs, or alcohol—may have noticeable effects on some youth.

Other temptations—such as inclinations to be cynical, power-hungry, or greedy—may not be so transparent, especially in a culture that sometimes rewards or celebrates succumbing to these enticements.

Temptation and Lent

The Lenten season offers us a time to turn away from temptation and see how Jesus' power over temptation can help us to live more fully in his grace. During this season, youth can develop a keener awareness of how they are tempted and how their desires control them. (The tradition of giving up something for Lent helps Christians deal with temptation. See page 57 for ideas and information.) Lent also gives youth the assurance that Christ will see them through their temptations, providing strength and comfort. And since youth, like all of us, will sometimes fail to overcome temptation, they should be reminded that in Christ they are forgiven.

How can youth learn to trust God when they encounter temptation?

Mission: Easter—Youth Programs & Ideas for Lent

First Sunday

Mission Plan

Activity	Supplies
Temptation TV	• markers • a markerboard or large sheet of paper • paper and writing utensils
In the Garden	• Bibles
In the Wilderness	• Bibles
Role-ing With the Punches	• copies of Tempting Roleplays handout (page 55)
Lead Us Not Into Temptation	• copies of the Lead Us Not Into Temptation handout (page 56) • pens or pencils
Temptation Talk	No supplies needed

Bible Study: Luke 4:1-13

You will need Bibles. Optional: different translations of the Bible.

Temptation: The First Sunday in Lent

You Will Need

- markers
- a markerboard or large sheet of paper
- paper and writing utensils for the youth to take notes about their show ideas

Temptation TV

Say: "In many respects, television shows mirror the temptations we face. Some shows may even present us with new temptations." Divide the large writing surface into two columns. Ask the youth to name the temptations that people their age face (such as drinking, putting down peers, overeating, not eating, and having sex). Write these examples in the left-hand column. Then ask the youth to name one television show that reflects each temptation. (For example, shows set in bars reflect the temptation to drink, and shows featuring promiscuous characters reflect the temptation to engage in irresponsible sexual behavior.)

Divide the youth into teams of three or four. (If you have fewer than five youth, have everyone work together as one group.) Ask each team to come up with a premise, a title, and main characters for two different types of shows (such as sitcoms, reality shows, crime dramas, and game shows). Each show should focus on a particular temptation that might entice viewers to tune in. A team might create a reality show about greed in which characters compete for a large sum of money. Another team might create a drama in which revenge and murder constantly tempt the characters.

Allow the groups five minutes to work. Then say: "Pretend I'm a television executive. I want you to 'pitch' your ideas to me. Try to convince me that your shows would entice viewers." One at a time, ask the teams to present their ideas. If time permits, have the youth vote on which shows they think would get the biggest ratings if the shows were on TV.

Say: "As we can see, we can easily think of ways to tempt people. Giving in to temptations—whether they come from television or from our friends at school—is just as easy if we don't trust God's plan for our lives. Today we will look at how Jesus overcame many of the same temptations we face and gave us an example of how God wants us to live."

You Will Need

- Bibles

In the Garden

Ask one volunteer to read aloud **Genesis 2:15-17**, and ask another to read aloud **Genesis 3:1-7**. Say: "These Scriptures speak to our weaknesses and our tendency to give in to temptation. This ancient story shows that human beings have always rebelled against God. Some interpreters feel that Adam and Eve gave in to pride; others think simple curiosity was to blame. At any rate, temptation has always been with us."

Mission: Easter—Youth Programs & Ideas for Lent

Ask:

✝ Why, do you think, did Adam and Eve give in to the temptation to eat from the tree of the knowledge of good and evil?

✝ What does this passage tell us about humans and temptation?

✝ What modern-day examples can you name that reflect these same human weaknesses, struggles, and temptations? (Encourage the youth to think of examples of letting one's curiosity get the best of him or her or acting wrongly to get ahead in life.)

In the Wilderness

Divide the youth into three groups. Assign each group one of the sections of Luke 4 below. (If you have a small number of youth, assign each youth a section; you may need to assign the same Scripture to more than one youth. If you have a large number of youth, divide them into six groups and give each Scripture to two groups.)

- Group One: **Luke 4:1-4** (temptation to turn stones to bread)

- Group Two: **Luke 4:5-8** (temptation of authority over the kingdoms of the world)

- Group Three: **Luke 4:9-13** (temptation of throwing himself from the pinnacle of the temple)

Instruct all of the groups to read Luke 4:1-13 in its entirety but to pay special attention to their assigned verses. Say: "Your group's assigned verses tell of a temptation that Jesus faced in the wilderness. Identify and discuss the temptation in your assigned verses. Then consider what temptations you might face that are similar to this temptation." (For example, the temptation to turn stones into bread would be similar to the temptation to scarf down unnecessary snacks just because they look tasty.) Give the groups about five minutes to read and discuss. Then have a representative from each group tell what examples his or her group came up with.

Role-ing With the Punches

Gather the youth in a circle, and distribute a copy of the Tempting Roleplays handout (page 55). Select three youth to roleplay in the center of the circle each of the characters described on the handout. Tell the rest of the youth that they will be listening to the characters' scenarios and will be invited to give advice to each of the characters.

Have each volunteer describe his or her situation. The volunteers may read aloud the descriptions of their characters written on the handout,

You Will Need
- Bibles

Suggestion: For ways to help youth deepen their understanding of the temptations Jesus faced, see the Bible Study on page 15.

You Will Need
- copies of Tempting Roleplays handout (page 55)

Temptation: The First Sunday in Lent

Remember These Key Points:

- Temptations come in different forms. What may tempt one person may not affect another.

- Some temptations come in the form of desire or peer pressure. Others may arise from deficiencies in our lives or from a lack of will or strength.

- Friends who support one another and hold one another accountable can help one another deal with temptation.

You Will Need
- copies of the Lead Us Not Into Temptation handout (page 56)
- pens or pencils

or they may creatively develop the character based on the descriptions. Then invite the youth on the outside of the circle one at a time come to the middle to offer advice to their struggling peer. Allow three or four youth to offer advice to each character.

Encourage the three characters to affirm advice that is helpful and to ask questions about advice they struggle with. After the youth have given advice to a character, give your own take on the situation.

After all three characters have presented their situations and listened to the advice of their peers, ask:

✝ What do you think drives these characters' temptations? peer pressure? low self-esteem? physical desire?

✝ What would have made these situations more realistic?

✝ What happens to someone's soul when he or she gives in to temptation?

Say: "These situations are based on real temptations that adolescents often struggle with. But in real life the situations are usually far more complex and the temptations much harder to overcome. Still, friends who listen, offer advice, and support you can help you resist even the most enticing temptations."

Lead Us Not Into Temptation

Distribute copies of the Lead Us Not Into Temptation handout (page 56). Read aloud **Luke 11:1-4** (The Lord's Prayer). Then give the youth about ten minutes to complete the handout. (Some youth may not feel comfortable answering some of the questions. Tell the youth that if they don't want to write down the answers to some questions they can just reflect on those questions.) When they have finished, go through the questions on the handout one at a time, allowing the youth to offer their thoughts and answers.

Temptation Talk

Say: "Temptation affects all of us, even when we don't notice it. Yet God has given us a strong advocate and example in Christ, who can help us overcome our weaknesses and move on when we fail. Let's ask God for help when we feel tempted, and forgiveness when we succumb to temptations." Then lead this closing prayer:

Dear God, we are so grateful that Jesus was made like us and that he was tempted and tested just as we are. And yet he did not sin but was faithful until death so that his strength and power could help us in our need. Help us to face our temptations in his love and remember his presence when we feel weak and powerless. In Jesus' name we pray. Amen.

Mission: Easter—Youth Programs & Ideas for Lent

Bible Study

Luke 4:1-13

You Will Need Bibles and copies of the Bible Dictionary (pages 75–80). Optional: different Bible translations and other reference materials.

Instruct the youth to read **Luke 4:1-13** (Jesus' temptation in the wilderness). Also, encourage the youth to look up the Old Testament verses Jesus cites when he responds to the devil (**Deuteronomy 8:3; 6:13, 16**) and to look up *wilderness* in the Bible Dictionary. Then instruct the youth to read **Matthew 4:1-11** and compare Matthew's version of the story to Luke's. If time permits, ask the youth to swap Bibles and read from different translations.

Ask:

✤ How did reading different versions and translations of this story affect your understanding of it?
✤ What are some of the similarities and differences between Luke's Gospel account (4:1-13) and Matthew's (4:1-11)? *(Matthew mentions angels helping Jesus; in Luke the devil departs until "an opportune time"; the tests vary slightly in order; and in Luke the devil claims authority over the world.)*

Say: "Jesus spent forty days in the wilderness where he was tested. The number *forty* is significant, because the Israelites spent forty years in the wilderness after being delivered from slavery in Egypt. Like Jesus, the Israelites were tested—they just didn't do as well. Let's look at where the Israelites went wrong." Ask a youth to read aloud **Numbers 14:1-4, 11-14, 19-23**. (You might select four youth to read: one to narrate, one to read God's lines, one to be Moses, and one to be the Israelites.)

Say: "Jesus succeeds where his forebears failed. Though Jesus was in the wilderness for forty days, not forty years, some Christians believe this story demonstrates that Jesus is the fulfillment of God's promise to Israel."

Ask:

✤ Why is the connection to the Israelites significant?
✤ Why else is this story significant for Christians? What lessons does it teach?
✤ What do you think of when you hear the word *wilderness?*

Some youth might associate *wilderness* with a vast forest or jungle. Say: "The wilderness that Jesus and the Israelites would have known was a desert that was perhaps similar to the deserts in the southwestern United States. This wilderness was hot, dry, rocky, and devoid of plant life." Ask:

✤ What hardships would a person face traveling through this type of wilderness?
✤ Where could you find food and water in this environment? Where would you sleep?

Say: "Now that you've examined this passage, take another look at the three tests." Ask:

✤ Which of these three tests do you think would have been most tempting?
✤ What do you think the devil was trying to accomplish in each test?
✤ How did Jesus respond to each test?

Ask the youth to think about how they have been tempted to either commit sinful acts or reject God's will. Challenge the youth to consider three temptations they face in everyday life. Then ask the teens to write these temptations on a slip of paper and keep the slip in their Bibles.

Say: "Jesus used Scripture to respond to each of the devil's tests. Likewise, Scripture can help you deal with your temptations. Keep your lists of temptations in your Bibles, and as you read the Bible keep an eye out for those passages that might help you deal with the temptations you're facing. Write the chapters and verses of these passages beside the appropriate temptations."

Temptation: The First Sunday in Lent

Second Sunday

Following Jesus: The Second Sunday in Lent

Key Verse: "If any want to become my followers, let them deny themselves and take up their cross and follow me" (**Mark 8:34b**).

Old Testament: **Genesis 12:1-4a**
(God calls Abram.)

New Testament: **Mark 8:31–9:1**
(Followers of Christ must take up their cross.)

The Sacrificial Life

For centuries, some Christians have "given up something for Lent." This idea may be familiar to some youth. Those unfamiliar with the tradition may find it either compelling or confusing, wondering, *What exactly are we called to give up? What true sacrifices must we make to be followers of Christ? How easy or difficult is the Christian life supposed to be?*

Christian sacrificial living begins by focusing on Jesus' life and death. Jesus offered his example, his teaching, and his life to us; now he asks us to give of ourselves for others. This form of discipleship requires reflection, strength, courage, and faith and leads us into a deeper relationship with Christ.

Many youth may not welcome the idea of sacrificing for others because our culture emphasizes competition, glorifies material comfort, and recognizes individual achievements. But giving up something for Lent can yield rewards. For example, giving up junk-food snacks might help a youth muster the discipline of eating healthier. The money he or she no longer feeds into vending machines or cash registers at fast food restaurants can be given to programs that assist hungry people. Giving up TV might allow a youth more time do volunteer work or to participate in church and school. Giving up putdowns benefits both the youth dishing out the insults and the recipients.

Of course, giving up something for Lent should affect a one's life for a long time after Easter comes and goes. Sacrifice helps us develop restraint, teaching us how much is too much and making us aware of how our resources might better be used. Thus we can find more productive ways to use our time, talents, and money. Living this way, we grow in our relationships with Christ, who calls us to "deny ourselves," or to give sacrificially for the benefit of others. So invite your youth to think about what they can give up and what they can better use in service to God and others.

For more information, see "Giving It Up for Lent" (page 57).

> **What must youth give up to follow Jesus?**

Mission: Easter—Youth Programs & Ideas for Lent

Second Sunday

Mission Plan

Activity	Supplies
It's in the News	• newspapers; magazines; conference, presbytery, or diocese newsletters; or news stories from websites
Abram's Example	• Bibles (of several translations if possible)
The Circle of Sacrifice	• an index card or small square of paper per youth • Bibles • prizes described on page 18
Giving It Up for Lent	• copies of Giving It Up for Lent handout (page 57) • Bible • index cards • pens or pencils
Circles of Influence	• copies of Circles of Influence handout (page 58) • pens or pencils
The Prayer of Saint Francis	No supplies needed

Bible Study: Genesis 12:1-5; Mark 8:31-9:1

You will need Bibles, copies of the Bible Dictionary (pages 75–80), and one small cross for each youth. Optional: a large cross, slips of paper, pens or pencils, chalk or marker, large writing surface.

Following Jesus: The Second Sunday in Lent

You Will Need

- newspapers; magazines; conference, presbytery, or diocese newsletters; or news stories from websites

Scan the sections beforehand to make sure each one includes an appropriate story.

You Will Need

- Bibles (of several translations if possible)

You Will Need

- an index card or small square of paper per youth
- Bibles
- small prizes for the entire group such as a dessert that can be split among many people
- individual prizes for the three winners such as Easter eggs containing candy or other items

Write the number 1 on one card, 2 on the next, and 3 on the next. Create the rest of the cards in the same way. Then shuffle the cards, making sure the deck has no consecutive numbers.

It's in the News

As the youth arrive, give each of them a couple sections of the newspaper. Instruct the youth to scan their sections of the paper for stories about persons who have made sacrifices (such as those who have helped clean up after a natural disaster, risked their lives to save others, or ministered to the homeless). Encourage the youth to "read between the lines" to discover sacrifices that are not obvious.

Once everyone has arrived, give the youth about five minutes to work. Then ask volunteers to talk about the examples of sacrifice they have found in the stories.

Abram's Example

Read aloud **Genesis 12:1-4** (God calls Abram). Then say, "Abram's story reminds us that being faithful to God is not always easy."

Ask:

✝ What were Abram and Sarai willing to sacrifice to obey God?

✝ How did God respond to Abram's faithfulness?

Say: "Abram's story shows us that while God often has extraordinary expectations, God has even greater promises. No matter how faithful we are to God, God is always more faithful to us."

The Circle of Sacrifice

Gather the youth in a circle. Hand each youth a card with a number on it. Have the youth hold their cards so that everyone can see them. Do not hand the numbers out in numerical order. Say: "I want you to get in numerical order, but I don't want anyone to move. To get in order, you may trade numbers with only the persons on your immediate left or right. If you can get in numerical order, I'll give everyone a prize and I'll give special prizes to the three players holding the consecutive numbers 1, 2, and 3. If you cannot get in numerical order, no one gets a prize."

The series of numbers can start anywhere in the circle and can go clockwise or counterclockwise, but they must be in order. If the group is to get in numerical order, some youth will have to sacrifice by trading a 1, 2, or 3 card. But if the youth hang on to these three cards, chances are that no one will get a prize.

Continue the game until the youth complete the task or until they become stuck. If the youth make a valiant effort and are willing to give up winning cards but are unable to complete the task in an

18

Mission: Easter—Youth Programs & Ideas for Lent

appropriate amount of time, award the group a prize but don't give out individual prizes. If they are successful, award a group prize and individual prizes for the three winners.

As the group enjoys its prize, read aloud **Luke 14:7-11** (the parable of the wedding banquet). Say: "As we have seen from this exercise, giving up a cherished place to someone else is not easy, especially when we think we might receive prestige, glory, or other rewards for that place."

Ask:

✞ How did it feel to trade a prize-winning card for the good of the group?

✞ How did it feel to receive a prize-winning card from someone else?

✞ When have you had to give up something or set aside personal goals for the good of the group or community?

Then say: "We often associate sacrifice with losing. But as Jesus and this exercise have shown us, when we are able to set aside personal interests and work together, we all win. Learning how to sacrifice is one way we understand the love of God expressed in the church, where all things are held in common."

Giving It Up for Lent

Distribute copies of Giving It Up for Lent handout (page 57). Ask for volunteers to read aloud the information on the handout, or have the youth read it silently on their own. Then say: "During Lent, Christians have traditionally made sacrifices for the good of others. Our goal in giving something up is not just self-discipline or personal satisfaction. Instead, giving up something for Lent allows us to show our devotion to God and to work for the good of others."

Hand out the index cards and pens or pencils. Invite one of the youth to read aloud **Mark 8:31–9:1** (followers of Christ must take up their cross). Then say: "Write down one thing you would be willing to sacrifice to be more faithful to Christ this Lenten season and one way you could use the time, money, or energy you save to serve others. Keep your commitment in your Bible, your purse or wallet, or your room as a reminder of your decision."

If time permits, offer a prayer of commitment, asking for faithfulness in making Lenten sacrifices.

Option

If you have fewer than six youth, provide four index cards for each youth. Write the letter A on four of the cards, the letter B on four of the cards, and so on. Shuffle the cards, and give each youth four cards.

Instruct the youth to trade cards, with the goal of everyone getting four of a kind. Tell the youth that if everyone ends up with four matching cards, the group will win a prize and the person holding four A's will win a special prize. The group can only win if players are willing to give up their "A cards." Conclude with the Scripture reading and questions for the rest of the Circle of Sacrifice activity. (Note: You may also use a standard card deck for this activity.)

You Will Need

- copies of Giving It Up for Lent handout (page 57)
- Bible
- index cards
- pens or pencils

Following Jesus: The Second Sunday in Lent

You Will Need
- copies of Circles of Influence handout (page 58)
- pens or pencils

Circles of Influence

Distribute copies of Circles of Influence handout (page 58). Say: "Please take a few minutes to consider the ways your life influences others and vice versa. Completing the handout will help you see how our discipleship affects many people in many ways."

Give youth time to work, and complete the handout on your own. Then discuss why certain people influence us and the responsibility that comes with having an influence over others.

The Prayer of Saint Francis

Close by praying together The Prayer of Saint Francis. Copy the prayer onto a large writing surface or hand out hymnals or prayer books that include the prayer.

The Prayer of Saint Francis

Lord, make me an instrument of thy peace;
where there is hatred, let me sow love;
where there is injury, pardon;
where there is doubt, faith;
where there is despair, hope;
where there is darkness, light;
and where there is sadness, joy.

O Divine Master,
grant that I may not so much seek
to be consoled as to console;
to be understood, as to understand;
to be loved, as to love;
for it is in giving that we receive,
it is in pardoning that we are pardoned,
and it is in dying that we are born to
eternal life.

Mission: Easter—Youth Programs & Ideas for Lent

Bible Study

Genesis 12:1-5; Mark 8:31–9:1

You Will Need *Bibles, copies of the Bible Dictionary (page 75–80) and one small cross for each youth, Optional: a large cross to display, slips of paper, pens or pencils, other reference materials, chalk or marker, and a large writing surface.*

Divide youth into small groups and instruct them to read **Genesis 12:1-9** (God calls Abram). Ask groups to locate on a map in the back of a Bible or in a Bible atlas where Abram and Sarai lived. Have them consult the Bible Dictionary to learn about Haran, Canaan, and the lands and cities through which Abram and Sarai traveled.

Then divide the youth into two groups by gender, and ask the following questions:

Boys: What concerns do you think Abram had when God asked him to leave Haran?

Girls: What concerns do you think Sarai had when God asked her to leave Haran?

Boys: How do you think Abram prepared himself for this journey?

Girls: How do you think Sarai prepared herself for this journey?

Boys: What kinds of sacrifices do you think Abram had to make as a man?

Girls: What kinds of sacrifices do you think Sarai had to make as a woman?

All: What impresses you most about Abram and Sarai's faith?

Divide the class into mixed groups of four or five. Have each group select one person to read aloud **Mark 8:31–9:1** (followers of Christ must take up their cross) while the others follow along. If you have a cross, bring it in to display during this portion of the lesson.

Say: "The cross is the most common symbol of the Christian faith. And in this passage, Jesus tells his followers they will have to take up their crosses if they wish to follow him."

Instruct the groups to discuss these questions (which you may write on a large writing surface):

✝ Why, do you think, does Jesus mention a cross as a mark of our discipleship?

✝ What do you think Jesus had in mind when he asked us to take up our crosses? What sacrifices might taking up our crosses involve?

✝ What do you think Jesus meant when he said we would gain our lives by losing them? When have you gained from losing something or giving up something?

✝ When do you have trouble making sacrifices for Christ? What do you hold on to that you know you should give up?

Ask one volunteer from each group to summarize his or her group's discussion. These volunteers do not need to give an answer to each question, but they should talk about what questions sparked the most discussion and what insight or conclusions the group was able to draw from the conversation.

Then instruct each youth to think of one sacrifice he or she can make not just for Lent but in the weeks, months, and years that follow. Tell the teens that anything from giving up soft drinks to overcoming jealousy are viable sacrifices. Then hand each youth a small cross, and say: "This cross is a reminder of the sacrifice to which you are committing. You can keep it in your pocket, wallet, purse, or anywhere you can see it and hold it on a regular basis." Suggest that the youth write down their sacrifices on a slip of paper so that they don't forget their commitments.

Close the Bible study by asking a volunteer to read aloud **Psalm 95:1-7a** (a psalm of praise) as a closing prayer.

Following Jesus: The Second Sunday in Lent

Third Sunday

Faithfulness: The Third Sunday in Lent

Key Verse: "Whoever is faithful in a very little is faithful also in much" (Luke 16:10a).

Old Testament: **Exodus 17:1-7** (The Israelites test God by demanding water.)

New Testament: **Luke 13:1-9** (Jesus tells the parable of the barren fig tree.)

The Aim Is Faithfulness

Many voices and attractions compete for our attention. An assortment of demands and appointments often fill our days. Sometimes a day of rest or a moment with God seems like a waste of time. The Lenten season calls us beyond these attachments and to God, the giver of life and the foundation of all existence.

Many youth find themselves divided: They are scholars, athletes, employees, artists, friends, sons and daughters, siblings, and . . . oh yeah, Christians. Homes, schools, athletic teams, and the workplace demand a lot from today's adolescents.

Because the church is so welcoming and forgiving, youth sometimes get the impression that church is the one part of their lives where nothing important is at stake. Missing sports practices often results in a player sitting on the bench or getting booted from the team. But a youth can go on a church's summer mission trip even if he or she never attended a youth fellowship meeting. And rarely will a youth be asked, "Have you read your Bible this week?

What keeps youth from being faithful disciples?

How much time have you been spending in prayer?" In the meantime, competition for teams, awards, and college admissions often leaves youth with little room in their schedules for discipleship.

But the aim of our lives is faithfulness, which means staying true to God's call and doing God's will in our daily lives. While youth and adults alike can express their faithfulness by making sacrifices during Lent, they can also commit to new forms of faithfulness, such as maintaining or initiating daily prayer and devotional practices to continue year round. During Lent, youth can also develop habits of service and outreach.

Jesus told many stories that illustrate the meaning of faithfulness and point to our need for faithful living, working, and resting. This session will highlight what faithfulness means for youth today and invite them to take further steps in their Lenten journeys with Christ, who asks that all of us be his faithful followers in a world full of conflicting voices and demands.

Recommended Resource: "Connecting Worship and Daily Living in Lent," by Daniel Benedict, from The General Board of Discipleship of The United Methodist Church (*www.gbod.org/worship/default_body.asp?act=reader&item_id=3864*)

Mission: Easter—Youth Programs & Ideas for Lent

Third Sunday

Mission Plan

Activity	Supplies
Grabby Greeting Cards	• construction paper • colored markers
Complaints, Complaints	• Bibles • a large writing surface • markers or chalk
Coming Events	• copies of the Coming Events handout (page 59) • pens or pencils • Bible
Lean on Me	No supplies needed
Being Fruitful	• Bibles
An Apple a Day	• one apple for every two youth

Bible Study: Exodus 17:1-7; Luke 13:1-9

You will need Bibles, copies of the Bible Dictionary (pages 75–80), paper, and writing utensils. Optional: other Bible dictionaries and concordances.

Faithfulness: The Third Sunday in Lent

You Will Need
- construction paper
- colored markers

Verses
- **Psalm 51:10-12** ("Create in me a clean heart.")
- **Psalm 119:1-3** (Happy are those who follow God's law.)
- **Matthew 5:10** ("Blessed are those who are persecuted.")
- **John 14:12-14** (Christ will do anything we ask for in his name.)
- **1 Corinthians 16:13-14** (Be courageous and strong.)
- **1 Timothy 6:11-12** (Pursue righteousness and faith.)

You Will Need
- Bibles
- a large writing surface
- markers or chalk

You Will Need
- copies of the Coming Events handout (page 59)
- pens or pencils
- Bible

Grabby Greeting Cards

As the youth arrive, hand each of them a sheet of construction paper and several colored markers. Instruct them each to create a greeting card featuring a favorite Bible verse. Encourage the teens to use verses that deal with staying faithful to God (such as the ones in the margin) and to surround their verses with appropriate artwork.

Allow the youth ten to fifteen minutes to work; then ask for volunteers to read aloud their verses, explain why they chose their verses, and present any artwork they have included. Encourage the youth to give their cards to someone who might need a bit of help or to keep the cards as reminders of their faith.

Option for Grabby Greeting Cards: Have the youth sketch a rough draft of their greeting cards, and ask them to do the rest as homework. Many youth have access to technology that will enable them to create professional-looking cards or e-cards. Youth who are familiar with various software applications may have an easier time expressing their creativity on the computer than on construction paper.

Complaints, Complaints

Ask a volunteer to read aloud **Exodus 17:1-7** (the Israelites test God by demanding water) while the others follow along. If the youth have different translations, encourage the teens to point out how their translations differ. Then ask:

✟ In this Scripture, what do the Israelites complain about? How do these complaints compromise their faith in God?

✟ How might people of faith better respond to difficult situations?

✟ What do you think the Israelites want God to do for them? Do you think their demands are reasonable? Why, or why not?

Ask the youth to brainstorm things people complain about. List these grievances on a large writing surface. Then say: "Many times, we fall into the trap of complaining about our circumstances or of blaming God for life's difficulties. Complaining is only human. But complaints often keep us from being faithful to God in difficult times."

Coming Events

Give each youth a copy of Coming Events handout (page 59) and a pen or pencil. Allow the youth five to ten minutes to work on the handout individually.

24

Mission: Easter—Youth Programs & Ideas for Lent

Then divide the group into teams of three or four and have the youth discuss in their teams how they answered the questions on the handout. Tell them to focus on the following questions:

✠ How do your spiritual goals relate to your other life goals? Will working toward your spiritual goals help you achieve your other goals? Explain.

✠ What can you do this week that will help you accomplish the goals you have listed?

✠ How can you remind yourself of your short-term goals? your long-term goals? How can you hold yourself accountable and make sure you are working toward your goals?

Once the discussion dies down, read aloud **Psalm 119:1-7** (happy are those who follow God's law). Say: "Lent is a good time to let go of bad habits, but it is also a great time to pick up new, good habits." Encourage the youth to keep a copy of their goals somewhere they will notice the goals each day (such as on their mirrors or beside their beds). Suggest that they also keep a copy in their Bibles.

Suggestion: Write these questions on a markerboard or large sheet of paper.

Lean on Me

Ask the youth to pair off. Then try one or both of these challenges requiring cooperation and trust:

Note: Communication and balance are essential to this activity.

1. Have the youth sit back to back on the floor with their arms locked. Ask each pair to stand up together.

2. Standing face to face and holding hands, ask each person in the pair to take a turn at lowering the other toward the floor, using only leverage and body weight as a guide.

Suggestions: Do the second challenge on a carpeted floor or a padded surface, and pair each youth with someone who is close to the youth's weight.

Then ask:

✠ What did you learn from this activity (or these activities)? *(Possible answers: cooperation and trust)*

✠ How is being faithful to God similar to cooperating with God?

✠ What might keep us from totally committing ourselves to God? *(Possible answers: fear, lack of effort, and giving in to temptation)*

Say: "Without cooperation and trust, many human relationships—whether in business, athletics, a family, or elsewhere—become strained. The same is true for our relationships with God. Cooperating with God is an act of faith. When we pray that God's 'will be done,' we open ourselves to the possibilities God has for us and turn our lives over to God instead of relying on our own wisdom and strength."

Faithfulness: The Third Sunday in Lent

You Will Need
• Bibles

Suggestion: Refer to the Bible Dictionary (pages 75–80) for more information on Pilate's sacrifices and the Tower of Siloam.

Being Fruitful

Ask a youth to read aloud **Luke 13:1-9** (Jesus tells the parable of the barren fig tree). Then say: "Jesus was fond of using stories and personal experience to teach us about God. This passage teaches two lessons on faithfulness." Ask:

✞ What message is Jesus teaching when he talks about Pilate's sacrifices and the Tower of Siloam?

✞ Why, do you think, do we humans have a tendency to compare ourselves with others when we evaluate our own lives?

Say: "Jesus often used stories about plants to teach us about the kingdom of God. In this parable, he spoke about a fig tree that was not producing fruit. It was going to be cut down, but the farmer wanted to save it." Ask:

✞ Why, do you think, did Jesus use this analogy of a fig tree to talk about human beings?

✞ What does this story teach us about God's patience?

✞ What does this story teach us about the rewards of faithfulness?

✞ What Christian disciplines can help us produce fruit for God?

Say: "Lent is a time of year when we can plant new seeds that will eventually grow more fruit. It is also a time when we should prune old branches that no longer bear fruit. This Lenten season, what practices and habits can you develop that will enable you to produce more fruit? What practices and habits do you need to give up?"

You Will Need
• one apple for every two youth

Beforehand, cut each apple into halves. Make sure that the seeds are visible.

An Apple a Day

Give each youth half of an apple. Then say: "Take a few moments to consider the apple. Like the fruit of a fig tree, an apple has seeds that can reproduce more fruit. But first these seeds must die, transform, and grow; only then will new fruit trees be produced. As long as apple trees bear fruit, this cycle of death and rebirth will continue."

Allow the students time to reflect. Then say: "Jesus asked his followers to produce fruit that would please to God. The way we live our lives is our fruit and our harvest for God. Sometimes we live unfaithfully and produce little. Other times, we live faithfully, producing fruits of mercy, helpfulness, joy, love, laughter, hopefulness, peace, or justice. Consider the kinds of seeds you are planting in your life, and then give thanks to God. As you taste this apple today, give thanks for the goodness and faithfulness God offers each of us. Amen."

Mission: Easter—Youth Programs & Ideas for Lent

Bible Study

Exodus 17:1-7; Luke 13:1-9

You Will Need *Bibles, copies of the Bible Dictionary (pages 75–80), paper, and writing utensils. Optional: other Bible dictionaries and concordances.*

Divide youth into groups of five or six. Have each group select someone to read aloud **Exodus 17:1-7** (the Israelites test God by demanding water). Then ask:

✝ What human frailties does the behavior of the ancient Israelites reflect?
✝ How does God respond to the people's unfaithfulness? What does this response say about God's nature?

Ask groups to read **Luke 13:1-9** (the parable of the barren fig tree). Say: "Jesus was fond of using parables and contemporary events as teaching tools."

Distribute paper, writing utensils, and copies of the Bible Dictionary (pages 75–80) and other available reference materials. Tell the groups to look up each of the terms *parable, Pontius Pilate,* and *the Tower of Siloam* and write a brief description of it. (If time is limited, assign each group one term.)

Give groups a few minutes to work then ask a member of each group to read aloud his or her group's descriptions. Then ask:

✝ Why, do you think, did Jesus use short fictional stories to teach lessons? How did his parables make his teaching more effective?
✝ What do you find most compelling about Jesus' teaching in this Scripture? What do you find most confusing?
✝ If Jesus were to teach a similar lesson to a crowd of people in our community today,

what events or examples do you think he would use as illustrations?
✝ What do you think Jesus wants us to learn from this parable?

Ask other youth to read aloud these Scriptures:

- **Matthew 3:10** (Trees that do not bear good fruit will be thrown in the fire.)
- **Matthew 7:15-20** (You will know a tree by its fruits.)
- **John 15:16** ("I appointed you to go and bear fruit.")
- **Galatians 5:22-23** (the fruit of the spirit)

> "[A man] said to the gardener, . . . 'For three years I have come looking for fruit on this fig tree, and still I find none. Cut it down!' . . . He replied, 'Sir, let it alone for one more year, until I dig around it and put manure on it. If it bears fruit next year, well and good; but if not, you can cut it down.' "
>
> (Luke 13:6b-9)

Say: "Trees bearing fruit was a powerful metaphor for Jesus and the early church. If you were to retell the parable of the fig tree to a contemporary audience, what metaphor might you use?"

Have the youth write contemporary parables that teach a lesson similar to the one Jesus teaches in the parable of the fig tree. Allow the youth to work individually or in groups of two or three. Give them plenty of time to work, then allow volunteers to tell their parables to the others.

Instruct youth to close their eyes and reflect on the following questions:

✝ What keeps you from being more faithful?
✝ What do you need to do now to deepen your commitment to God?

Close in prayer, asking God to give the youth strength to honor their commitments to God and to remain faithful in any situation.

Faithfulness: The Third Sunday in Lent

Fourth Sunday

Calling: The Fourth Sunday in Lent

Key Verse: "Rejoice with me, for I have found my sheep that was lost" (Luke 15:6b).

Old Testament: 1 Samuel 16:1-13 (David is anointed as king.)

New Testament: Luke 15:1-3, 11b-32 (Jesus tells the parable of the prodigal son.)

When God Calls

Today's lesson offers two of the richest texts in the Bible: the story of the calling of the boy David to be king of Israel and Jesus' parable of the prodigal son whom his gracious father received. Both of these stories contain powerful lessons for youth and provide insight about God's grace, reflected during Lent through the grace of Jesus Christ.

Like the prophet Jeremiah, who was called to prophesy when he was only a youth, young people have been used by God throughout the ages to lead, bless, and give witness to God's grace and mercy. David was just a shepherd boy when God chose him from among his stronger and more mature brothers to become king of Israel. As the prophet Samuel noted, God looks upon the heart of a person rather than on the outward appearance. (See 1 Samuel 16:7.)

Jesus' famous parable of the prodigal speaks to those times in a young person's life when he or she has drifted away from God but still feels the powerful call to return home. The forgiving father awaits the wayward child with welcoming arms and a gracious heart. However, the prodigal's brother, a faithful and obedient son, cannot understand his father's gracious acceptance of the rebellious son.

Like the prodigal son and David, youth feel and respond to God's call in various ways. Some run from the call, while others eagerly spend time in prayer awaiting God's guidance. Yet each of your youth can discover some part of God's plan for his or her life. Discerning this plan, a crucial step along one's walk with God, is the goal of Christian discipleship.

Throughout much of the church's history, the Lenten season has been a time to welcome new members and to allow existing members to renew their commitments to the faith. Many churches still hold catechism or confirmation classes during Lent, and most hold special Lenten Bible studies. These programs affirm that every believer is an important part of God's family. Teaching young confirmands, adult converts, and long-time church members about our faith story and about opportunities for service within the church helps them to realize their role in the body of Christ and what God is calling them to do.

This Lenten lesson offers youth the chance to explore the ways God has chosen them, as well as the hope of exploring more deeply God's plan for their lives. God calls not only shepherd boys and prodigals but also teenage team captains, honor students, class clowns, and Internet junkies to faithful service and discipleship.

> **What potential and promise might God see in our youth?**

28

Mission: Easter—Youth Programs & Ideas for Lent

Fourth Sunday

Mission Plan

Activity	Supplies
<u>Great Accomplishments</u>	No supplies needed
<u>What? . . . God Use Me?</u>	• copies of What? . . . God Use *Me?* handout (page 60) • pens or pencils
<u>David Dynamics</u>	• Bibles
<u>Prodigal Pantomime</u>	• a Bible • hats and T-shirts to differentiate roles (optional)
<u>Homecoming</u>	• basic party supplies, most of which can be purchased at a dollar store
<u>Here Am I</u>	• a Bible • copies of What? . . . God Use *Me?* handout (page 60) (optional)

> ### <u>Bible Study: Luke 15:1-3, 11b-32</u>
>
> You will need Bibles and copies of the Bible Dictionary (pages 75–80). Optional: other Bible dictionaries and concordances, an audio recording of the Gospel of Luke, and a CD or cassette player.

Calling: The Fourth Sunday in Lent

Great Accomplishments

Ask persons in the group to each quickly find a partner. Tell them that partners will change often. If you have an odd number of youth, be someone's partner.

Then say: "Think about one or two great accomplishments in your life. Perhaps these accomplishments seem small or silly to you. However, if you consider something you've done an important milestone in your life I would like you to tell your partner about it. Take a minute to tell your partner about your accomplishments and listen while your partner tells you his or hers. When I say, 'Switch,' find another partner and repeat the activity."

Allow enough time for each person to switch partners three or four times. Then gather the group in a circle and ask:

✞ How much ease or difficulty did you have talking about your accomplishments?

✞ How was God involved in your greatest accomplishments?

Say: "Today's session looks at God's call. All of us have achievements to be proud of, and all of us have done things we'd like to forget. More importantly, all of us have promise and potential, and God has a plan for each of our lives."

You Will Need
- copies of What? . . . God Use *Me?* handout (page 60)
- pens or pencils

What?...God Use Me?

Distribute copies of What? . . . God Use *Me?* handout (page 60) and pens or pencils. Allow the youth ten or fifteen minutes to complete the handout and read the biblical reflections. Then ask:

✞ What did you learn about yourself from this activity?

✞ Why are our gifts and abilities important to God? to others?

✞ What does this activity tell us about the ways God can use us?

Ask a volunteer to lead the Heart Prayer at the bottom of the handout, or save this prayer for your closing.

You Will Need
- Bibles

David Dynamics

Ask a volunteer to read aloud **1 Samuel 16:1-13** (David is anointed king) while the others follow along. Then ask:

✞ Why was Samuel hesitant to look for a new king? When have fears and past failures kept you from boldly following God's lead?

30   **Mission: Easter—Youth Programs & Ideas for Lent**

✜ What do you think Samuel was looking for in a king? What were God's criteria for a new leader?

✜ When have you felt like the one "left to tend the sheep"? What might God see in you that others might not see in you? What might God see in you that God might not find in others?

Say: "David's story proves that God calls people of all ages and backgrounds. Because of his experience with Saul, Samuel was skeptical of anointing a new king, regardless of whom God would choose. And conventional wisdom would say that David was the least likely of Jesse's sons to be anointed king. Yet God chose David, the youngest son, the one left behind to tend the sheep."

Prodigal Pantomime

Do a pantomime performance of **Luke 15:11-32** (the parable of the prodigal son. Assign the parts below. (Involve every youth if possible.)

Necessary

- Narrator (the only speaker; reads the text from the Bible)
- The father
- The younger son
- The older son

Optional

- People in the distant country who party with the younger son
- The citizen for whom the younger son works
- The pigs the younger son feeds
- The father's servants

You Will Need
- a Bible
- hats and T-shirts to differentiate roles (optional)

Hand a Bible to the narrator, and tell him or her to read **Luke 15:11-32** aloud while the others act out their parts silently. Encourage the youth to dramatize the events. After the presentation, ask:

✜ To which of the two sons do you most relate? Why?

✜ Do you think what the father did was fair to the older brother? Why, or why not?

✜ If we know that God will celebrate our return, why shouldn't we go off and live recklessly for a while?

✜ What does this story tell us about God? about ourselves? about our attitudes toward others?

Say: "The twist in the parable of the prodigal son involves the role of the older brother. Through this character, Jesus demonstrates that just as God rejoices when someone repents and restores his or her relationship with God we should all celebrate when one of our lost siblings returns home. Jesus also uses the older son to remind us that God's grace is always available for us to claim."

Calling: The Fourth Sunday in Lent

You Will Need
- basic party supplies, most of which can be purchased at a dollar store

Note: God's "welcome-home parties" may include renewing one's faith after a time of doubt or struggle, overcoming negative or destructive behaviors, finally being able to forgive a loved one against whom one has held a grudge, and so on.

You Will Need
- a Bible
- copies of What? . . . God Use *Me?* handout (page 60) (optional)

Homecoming

Say: "The prodigal son's story speaks in several ways about our relationships with God and with one another. It talks about our human condition of alienation from God and others, and it illustrates God's redeeming love."

Hand out the party supplies, and ask the youth to create a festive atmosphere to celebrate the drama of God's redemption. If you have enough youth, divide them into teams and ask each team to oversee a particular aspect of the party, such as décor, table setting, menu, and music. Ask the youth to choose songs, colors, and so forth that would celebrate God's redeeming love. Allow the youth some time at the end to explain their choices.

As time allows, challenge the class with the following questions:

✝ When have you had one of God's "welcome-home parties"? How did it make you feel?

✝ When have you had a chance to celebrate someone else's "welcome-home party"? Did you celebrate joyously, or did you harbor feelings of jealousy like the prodigal's older brother did?

✝ What sights, sounds, words, or stories remind you of God's redeeming love (God's ongoing welcome-home party)?

Close by saying: "Like the prodigal son, we often find ourselves in the 'far country' of doubt, self-centeredness, or apathy. But when we hear God's call to come home and reconnect with our faith and our God, there is joy. Let us never forget that God provides many opportunities for us to turn our lives around, seek God's help, and celebrate the joy of God's undying love."

Here Am I

Gather the youth in a circle, and read aloud **Isaiah 6:8** ("Here I am; send me!"). Invite the youth to bow their heads in prayer. Then go around the circle and allow each youth to say a brief prayer asking for God's help in discerning his or her call, giving thanks for the plan God has for his or her life; or asking forgiveness for going astray. (The youth may pray silently if they would like.) When each youth is finished, have everyone say in unison, "God, I'm ready to come home."

If you wish, close by saying the Heart Prayer (page 60).

Mission: Easter—Youth Programs & Ideas for Lent

Bible Study

Luke 15:1-3, 11b-32

You Will Need *Bibles and copies of the Bible Dictionary (pages 75–80). Optional: other Bible dictionaries and concordances, an audio Bible, and a CD player.* (NRSV New Testament on CD *from World Publishing, Inc. is available at* www.Cokesbury.com; *ISBN 0-529-11493-3.*)

Begin by asking the youth to close their eyes and reflect on the following questions:

✝ When in your life have you felt like running away from home or escaping from your day-to-day life? What prompted these feelings?
✝ When have you felt alienated from God?

Allow plenty of time for contemplation. Then say: "A prodigal is someone who is rebellious by nature and sets out to discover life on his or her own. While this parable is commonly called 'the parable of the prodigal son,' some have called it 'the parable of the loving father' or the 'parable of the elder son,' because this parable tells three stories about our relationships with God."

Ask a volunteer to read aloud **Luke 15:1-3, 11b-32** (the parable of the prodigal son) while the other youth listen closely or with their eyes closed, or play an audio version of the Scripture on CD. Listening to parables can stimulate one's imagination. Afterward, ask:

✝ What characteristics or attributes does the younger son exhibit in this story?
✝ How do you think the younger son felt before he left home? soon after he left? when he was hungry and forced to work? when he decided to return? when he saw his father on the road?
✝ What do you think the father was doing during the son's absence?

After this discussion about the younger son, say: "Of course, another son is mentioned in this parable: the older son. In first-century Jewish society, the eldest son had many responsibilities, as well as blessings. As the firstborn, the oldest boy would receive the father's blessing and often the entire estate when the father died. But the oldest also had the responsibility of caring for his mother, providing for other family members (including women and children of the extended family), and making sure all members of the family had proper burials. Keep all of this information in mind as we consider how this son reacted to the return of his wasteful brother."

If your group needs to hear **Luke 15:25-32** again, reread or listen to the Scripture. Then ask:

✝ How might the older son's feelings and complaints be justified?
✝ What characteristics does the father demonstrate in his response to the older son? How do the father's words reflect God?
✝ How does the father demonstrate equal love for both of his sons? Do you think the father loves his two sons differently? Explain.

Say: "Jesus told this parable in response to those who were condemning and questioning him because he ate and associated with people considered sinful. The story of the prodigal, his father, and his brother reveals much about our desire to take life into our own hands and our tendency to envy others. But the story reveals even more about God's nature." Ask:

✝ What does this parable tells us about ourselves? about our relationships with one another?
✝ What does it tell us about God's love?

Close with these reflective questions, which the youth need not answer aloud:

✝ Where do you see yourself most clearly in this story? at home waiting for the prodigal? wandering? ready to come home? jealous of the rebellious sibling who returned?
✝ How do you see jealousy or arrogance at work in yourself? in our church? in our society?

Close with a silent prayer, inviting the youth to receive God's redeeming love. Remind the youth that God is always ready and willing to forgive and receive those who wish to come home.

Calling: The Fourth Sunday in Lent

Fifth Sunday

Devotion: The Fifth Sunday in Lent

Key Verse: "Then I heard the voice of the Lord saying, 'Whom shall I send, and who will go for us?' And I said, 'Here am I; send me!' " (**Isaiah 6:8**).

Old Testament: Isaiah 43:16-21 ("Do not remember the former things. . . . I am about to do a new thing.")

New Testament: John 12:1-8 (Mary of Bethany anoints Jesus.)

Expressing Devotion to God

The idea of devotion resonates with many youth. Teens who participate in athletics, music, theater, academic competitions, scouting, community organizations, and school clubs know that contributing to these groups requires a commitment of time, effort, and energy. Many adolescents must also devote themselves to managing their time so that they can effectively juggle schoolwork, extracurricular activities, church activities, jobs, and anything else they might be involved in.

Many youth know plenty about devotion. Your job is to help them become more fully devoted disciples of Jesus Christ. Devotion to God through Christ won't result in immediate, tangible results such as good grades, trophies, or paychecks; and it won't end with a graduation, a championship game, or retirement. God asks for a lifetime commitment that doesn't even stop for breaks, vacations, or off-seasons.

Through the classic disciplines of the church—prayer, Scripture reading, service, and worship—youth can develop devotional habits that will strengthen their relationships with God. By using their imaginations to perceive the "new thing" that God is doing (Isaiah 43:19), and not settling into tradition and routine worship, youth can help the church as a whole discover creative movements of the Spirit and new directions for Christian devotion.

The Lenten season gives youth manifold opportunities to deepen their devotion to God and to understand more fully the meanings of discipleship, sacrifice, and dedication. Early Christians expressed their devotion by abstaining from certain foods and practices and by rededicating themselves to Christ. While the Lenten fast lasted forty days (excluding Sundays), these devoted disciples hoped that their dedication during Lent would renew and strengthen their faith for the rest of the year. Many Christians today still find value in these practices of devotion.

> **How can youth express their devotion to God?**

Assisted by the wisdom of the prophets of ancient Israel and Judah and the witness of the early Christian evangelists, youth can chart out their paths of discipleship that leads to eternal life. They can find their places in the old and neverending story of their faith.

Mission: Easter—Youth Programs & Ideas for Lent

Fifth Sunday

Mission Plan

Activity	Supplies
<u>Team Spirit</u>	• a large writing surface • chalk or a marker • paper • pens or pencils
<u>Living With Complete Sentences</u>	No supplies needed
<u>A Prophet's Praise</u>	• Bibles • a large writing surface • chalk or a marker.
<u>God Stuff</u>	• Bibles • copies of God Stuff handout (page 61) • pens or pencils
<u>Pleasing Fragrances</u>	• scented candles, incense sticks, or aroma sprays • Bibles • a bouquet of flowers (optional)
<u>Worship Workshop</u>	• a Bible

<u>Bible Study: John 12:1-8</u>

You will need Bibles and copies of the Bible Dictionary (pages 75–80).
Optional: other Bible dictionaries and concordances

Devotion: The Fifth Sunday in Lent

You Will Need
- a large writing surface
- chalk or a marker
- paper
- pens or pencils

Beforehand, on a large writing surface list these games and game descriptions, leaving room for some more descriptions:

✢ The Pole-Sitting Bowl (teams compete in marathon pole-sitting)

✢ The Lawn Biathlon (teams compete in lawn fertilizing and mowing)

✢ The Butler's Cup (teams compete in a housecleaning tournament)

✢ The Light-Bulb Race (teams compete to screw in the most light bulbs)

✢ The TV Triathlon (teams compete in chip eating, soda drinking, and marathon TV watching)

- I do my best thinking when . . .
- No one is better than me at . . .
- I am most committed to . . .
- What I most enjoy is . . .
- My ultimate life goal is . . .
- I am most committed to . . .
- I pay attention to issues of . . .
- The movie about my life would be titled . . .
- I am most devoted to . . .

Team Spirit

Divide the youth into teams of four or five. (If you have fewer than eight youth, everyone can work as one team.) Show the youth the game descriptions, and allow each team to choose one of the off-the-wall team "sports" or one of their own. On the large writing surface, list the other "sports" the youth come up with.

Say: "Each team must determine a game plan for its event. This game plan should outline strategies for competition and the training and practice you will need to compete successfully. Be sure to include everyone on the team and have fun planning your winning strategy."

Hand out paper and pens or pencils to each team. Give the teams about five minutes to discuss. Then have representatives from each team go over their teams' game plans. Ask:

✢ What commitments would a member of your team need to make to be successful at this sport?

✢ What disciplines or practices would help an athlete perform up to his or her potential in your sport?

✢ How might the church be compared to a sports team? Is the church competing in any games or competitions? Explain.

Then say: "During Lent our faith is strengthened through our participation in traditional practices. This lesson will help us get a better idea of our discipleship 'game plan' for the Lenten season."

Living With Complete Sentences

Gather the youth in a circle. Move quickly around the circle, asking each youth to complete one of the sentences listed in the margin before moving on to the next person and asking him or her to complete the next sentence. This activity is most effective when the participants offer the first answer that comes to mind. If a youth hesitates more than five seconds, move to the next person. (You may go around the circle multiple times.) Be clear that the youth do not have to complete any sentences they are uncomfortable completing.

When you have finished, say: "Life often moves quickly, and it doesn't always give us time to think about our goals and convictions. Lent is a time to stop, consider our devotion to Christ, and re-commit ourselves to discipleship."

Give the youth a some time to sit in silence and reflect on what they consider truly important and what they might need to change. Allow volunteers to talk about any insight they gained from the time they spent in silence.

Mission: Easter—Youth Programs & Ideas for Lent

A Prophet's Praise

Ask a volunteer to read aloud **Isaiah 43:16-21** ("Do not remember the former things. . . . I am about to do a new thing") while the others follow along. Say: "The Old Testament prophets demanded that their nation demonstrate God's justice and mercy. These prophets were deeply devoted to God and often spoke of God's wonders and praise." Ask:

✝ How does this prophet praise God in this Scripture? How does Isaiah's praise of God make his message more powerful?

✝ Isaiah tells the people that God is "about to do a new thing." What new thing does Isaiah envision God doing?

✝ Why, do you think, does God want the people not to "remember the former things or consider the things of old"? Why does God need to do something new?

Say: "Using our imaginations, a gift from God, can be one form of devotion. God may lead us toward new ways of worshiping or serving others that will touch people whom our current ministries aren't reaching." Ask:

✝ What new things might God be asking us to do as a youth group or congregation? Use your imaginations.

Record the teens' ideas on a large writing surface. Then work with the youth to select one or two ideas to which they feel the congregation or youth group should commit. If time permits, help the youth implement a game plan for bringing these ideas to fruition.

You Will Need
- Bibles
- a large writing surface
- chalk or a marker

God Stuff

Distribute copies of God Stuff handout (page 61). This activity will help the teens become more aware of the diversity of traditions and practices that Christians have used to express their devotion to God. God Stuff will challenge the youth to find ways to incorporate these disciplines into their lives.

Work through the handout with the youth. Ask for volunteers to read aloud the appropriate Scriptures. Help the youth to think of ways in which the various disciplines listed on the handout can strengthen faith.

Say: "Though Christians worship in many different ways and we sometimes disagree on some aspects of the faith, all Christians share a sacred Scripture and a belief in a Creator who has redeemed us through Jesus Christ. We also believe that the church is the manifestation of Christ's body in the world today."

You Will Need
- copies of God Stuff handout (page 61)
- pens or pencils

Devotion: The Fifth Sunday in Lent

You Will Need
- scented candles, incense sticks, or aroma sprays
- Bibles
- a bouquet of flowers (optional)

Beforehand, ask the youth if they are allergic to certain elements.

You Will Need
- a Bible

Components of a Worship Service
- Call to worship: a poem, responsive reading, or Scripture passage
- Scripture lesson: a reading or readings from the Bible followed by a brief message
- Music: hymns, praise songs, a solo, or chants
- Closing prayer: a short or responsive prayer given by one person

Pleasing Fragrances

Option: Place a bouquet of flowers in the center of your meeting space, and ask the youth to take in the various scents as you read aloud **Psalm 45:6-8a** ("Your throne, O God, endures forever and ever").

Light the candle or incense sticks, or spray the aroma sprays. Read aloud **John 12:1-8** (Mary anoints Jesus). Say: "Protestant churches rarely use smells as a means of invoking God's spirit or connecting with God. However, today's Gospel lesson invites the use of pleasing aromas." Ask:

✤ How can our senses connect us with God?

✤ We often perceive sights, sounds, and tastes in worship. How can we use our senses of smell and touch as we worship God?

If time permits, refer to the multisensory worship ideas on pages 71–72.

Worship Workshop

Say: "Devotion to Christ involves our adoration, which often involves a group or community of Christians. Worship usually takes place on Sunday mornings, but it can happen spontaneously in our lives when we pray, contemplate, and sing of the glories and mercies of God." Divide the youth into four groups, and ask each group to plan one of the components of a short worship service listed in the margin. (If the youth have trouble finding Scriptures, suggest Scriptures related to this lesson, such as **Psalm 45:6-8a; Isaiah 42:10-13; 43:16-21;** or **John 12:1-8**.)

If you have a small number of youth, divide them into two groups and assign each group two of the assignments. If you have a large number of youth, form additional groups to work on incorporating the senses of smell and touch into the service.

Mission: Easter—Youth Programs & Ideas for Lent

Bible Study

John 12:1-8

You Will Need: *Bibles and copies of the Bible Dictionary (pages 75–80). Optional: other Bible dictionaries and concordances.*

Read aloud **John 11:55-57**. Say: "Tension develops between Jesus and his closest followers shortly before the events of today's Scripture. Jesus' disciples suspected that their teacher would be in danger if he made the trip to Jerusalem for the Passover festival.

"By traveling to Jerusalem, Jesus demonstrates great courage and faith. He is devoted to the purpose he has been called to fulfill though he knows the difficulties to come." Ask:

✝ When have you had to muster great courage?
✝ How was your courage rewarded?

If you have access to concordances, full Bible dictionaries, and Bible atlases, provide them along with copies of the Bible Dictionary (pages 75–80). Invite a volunteer to read aloud **John 12:1-8** (Mary anoints Jesus). Have the youth pair off, and assign each pair one of the following questions:

✝ Why was the Passover festival important to a Jew such as Jesus?
✝ Where is Bethany, and why is this town important?
✝ Who was Lazarus, and why was he significant in Jesus' life?
✝ Who were Mary and Martha?
✝ What details can you find about Judas Iscariot?
✝ How costly was the ointment in this Scripture? In other words, what was 300 denari worth?

Allow each pair to present what it has learned, and fill in the gaps, using the Leader Information to the right.

Then divide youth into groups of three or four for discussion. Ask:

✝ What acts of worship or devotion does **John 12:1-8** reflect?

✝ To whom in this passage do you most relate? Why?
✝ What do you think of Judas Iscariot's response to Mary's actions? Did he have a point? Explain.
✝ What do you think Jesus meant by saying the poor will always be with us?

Then gather all of the youth in a circle and ask:

✝ What valuable possessions would you be willing to offer to Christ?
✝ How is making a financial sacrifice an act of devotion?
✝ How can devotion to Jesus change our lives?

To close say: "As we depart today, may we be reminded of the call to serve, trust, and give. God desires our best, and when we give our best to God we are growing in our discipleship."

Leader Information: The people mentioned in this passage were of great importance to Jesus. He wept at the tomb of his close friend Lazarus before raising him from the dead. The other Gospels describe Martha as a committed follower of Jesus who provides for the needs of Jesus and his followers. Mary is a deeply spiritual person who sacrifices the expensive ointment she used to anoint Jesus. Mary's anointing of Jesus is a sign that he is the Messiah (which means "the anointed one") and that he will soon die (as bodies were anointed for burial in Jewish custom).

The events in this Scripture took place around Passover, Judaism's greatest festival and holy day. Passover is a memorial of the Israelites' passage from Egypt to freedom and from death to life. In Bethany, Jesus was the guest of honor and would have likely presided over the meal. Bethany's close proximity to Jerusalem gives us a sense of danger and foreboding.

Judas Iscariot will later betray Jesus for money, but we cannot forget that Judas is a trusted disciple with an important job: keeping the common money needed for the survival of the itinerant group from Galilee led by Jesus.

Devotion: The Fifth Sunday in Lent

Palm Sunday

Sacrifice: Palm Sunday

Key Verse: "For a little while you have had to suffer various trials, so that the genuineness of your faith . . . may be found to result in praise and glory and honor when Jesus Christ is revealed" (**1 Peter 1:6b-7**).

Old Testament: **Isaiah 50:4-9**

(God's servant is glorified for enduring suffering.)

New Testament: **Matthew 27:11-54**

(Jesus' is tried and crucified.)

Enduring Tests of Faith

Palm Sunday marks the beginning of the holiest week in the Christian tradition. Holy Week, as it is appropriately called, recognizes the period of time beginning with Jesus' entry into Jerusalem and concluding with his resurrection. Holy Week is punctuated with special worship moments commemorating the Last Supper (Maundy Thursday), the Crucifixion (Good Friday) and, of course, Jesus' resurrection (Easter).

Palm Sunday gets its name from the tree branches laid down in front of Jesus by the people celebrating his arrival in Jerusalem. Though it commemorates the joyous celebration of Jesus coming to town, this day has also traditionally been the Sunday when churches remember the trials and the passion of Jesus. In fact, Christians sometimes call Palm Sunday "Passion Sunday." While this day is often marked by handing out fronds from palm branches, many Palm Sunday services include the reading of a Passion narrative—the story of Jesus' trial and execution—from one of the Gospels.

For youth who often feel tested by their peers and the culture they live in, Jesus' trial may hold particular interest. At his trial, Jesus gave the ultimate testimony, proving his faithfulness even to the point of death. The English words *test*, *testimony*, and *testament* come from the same Latin root associated with "giving witness." As Christians, we cannot disassociate our testimony, the way we live out our faith, from the tests we endure. Likewise, the Old and New Testaments are written witnesses of the tests that living witnesses have endured for their faith.

Renowned youth ministry scholar Kenda Creasy Dean says that today's youth are "dying for something worth dying for" and that following Christ is "unavoidably dangerous." She charges those of us who minister to youth to affirm that testifying and enduring tests for Christ is OK and that it is worth the risk.*

When have you been put on trial?

Taking a closer look at Jesus' trial should challenge youth to consider the tests and trials they face (or will face) as Jesus' followers. This session aims to take youth on a Holy Week journey with Christ and give them the strength and confidence to deal with their tests and trials in a Christlike manner. By remaining faithful during the most difficult times, youth can give powerful testimony about Christ's love and presence.

*From *Practicing Passion: Youth and the Quest for a Passionate Church* by Kenda Creasy Dean (Wm. B. Eerdmans, 2004), pages 30–36.

Mission: Easter—Youth Programs & Ideas for Lent

Palm Sunday

Mission Plan

Activity	Supplies
<u>Palms Up!</u>	• palm fronds or green, leafy branches • Bibles
<u>Trials and Tribulations</u>	• Bibles
<u>Stations of the Trial</u>	• Bibles • copies of Stations of the Trial handout (page 63) • markers (optional) • small writing surfaces (optional)
<u>Foot Washing</u>	• a Bible • one wash cloth for each youth • one towel for each youth • a water basin • a pitcher (optional)
<u>Standing Trial</u>	• chairs
<u>Closing Reflection</u>	• a Bible

<u>Bible Study: Matthew 27:11-16</u>

You will need Bibles and one small cross for each youth. Optional: several translations of the Bible, other Bible dictionaries, concordances, a large writing surface, and chalk or a marker.

Sacrifice: Palm Sunday

You Will Need
- palm fronds or green, leafy branches
- Bibles

Beforehand, obtain palm fronds or leafy green branches from your local florist (these are generally inexpensive).

In lieu of actual palm fronds or leafy branches, you could bring small towels that youth could wave in the air.

You Will Need
- Bibles

Palms Up!

As the youth arrive, hand each one a frond or branch. Ask a volunteer to read aloud **John 12:12-16** (Jesus' triumphant entry into Jerusalem) while the others follow along.

Then say: "Today is Palm Sunday, a day when Christians around the world remember Jesus' triumphant arrival in Jerusalem for the Passover festival. Today is also the first day of Holy Week, the week when we ritually observe Jesus' last supper, mourn his crucifixion, and celebrate his resurrection.

"On the surface, Jesus' entry into the city may seem like a long, overdue celebration of the Messiah. But the occasion was also dangerous for Jesus. Why? The symbol of the palm branch has always been closely tied to the nation of Israel, and in Jesus' day it represented national independence from the Romans. By chanting hosannas, the people were welcoming Jesus as if they expected him to soon be king, a clear sign of insurrection to any Romans who might have been watching. The crowd was excited, but to Jesus the celebration was one of the most dangerous moments of his life."

Invite the youth to sit in a circle and wave their palms. Go around the circle, and give each youth a chance to explain why he or she would welcome Jesus as king. Then say: "Even though Jesus was never a king in the earthly sense, Christians call him the 'king of kings.' How does Jesus compare with an earthly king or other world leader?"

Trials and Tribulations

Divide the youth into groups of three or four. (If you have fewer than six youth, do this activity as a single group.) Say: "Many times in life, we endure stress, uncertainty, or struggle. Sometimes these experiences do not relate to faith. Other times, however, we feel as though our faith, our beliefs, or our relationships with God are being called into question or put on trial." Ask:

✠ When has your faith been put to the test? How did you react?

✠ How do challenges to your faith strengthen it? How do they weaken it?

✠ Which Christian beliefs, do you think, are most often put to the test?

✠ What Christian principles are most difficult to live up to? Why?

Give each group time to read **Matthew 27:11-26** (Jesus' trial and crucifixion). Then ask:

✠ What tests and trials did Jesus have to endure?

✝ How is Jesus' faithfulness impressive in this Scripture? How can we learn from and follow his example?

Say: "None of us is as strong or faithful as Jesus. And none of us has been through the trials Jesus suffered that spring in Jerusalem. Jesus' example gives us a goal and motivation to reach that goal: If Jesus could hold fast to his faith and convictions in the face of certain suffering and death, we can hold fast to our faith and convictions in the face of ridicule and peer pressure."

Stations of the Trial

Say: "For centuries, Christians have observed the Holy Week tradition of walking the Stations of the Cross. Although this tradition has not always been observed by Protestants, walking the stations lets us recognize Jesus' suffering and death in a tangible way. By symbolically walking to the cross with him and remembering his passion, we become one in his suffering, death, and resurrection.

"Today, however, we will walk the stations of the trial with Jesus as our guide and try to identify more fully with his trials and suffering."

Distribute Bibles and copies of Stations of the Trial handout (page 63), and divide the youth into five groups. Have each group start at a different one of the five stations. At each station, the groups will read the appropriate Scripture and answer the appropriate question printed on the handout. Give the groups a few minutes at each station, then instruct them to rotate. (If you have fewer than eight youth, have all of the youth walk from station to station, read the appropriate Scripture, and answer the appropriate question together.)

Select a youth to read the Litany of Love printed on the handout, and close with the litany.

You Will Need
- Bibles
- copies of Stations of the Trial handout (page 63)
- markers (optional)
- small writing surfaces (optional)

Beforehand, select five locations in your church building as "stations." Good locations might be in the sanctuary, near the altar, by a stained glass window, in a prayer chapel, or in a dark room. Optional: Post signs on walls at various places in the church.

Foot Washing

If you feel that your group is particularly close or receptive to a more intimate type of remembrance, do a memorial foot washing.

Begin by asking a youth to read aloud **John 13:1-17** (Jesus' washes his disciples' feet). Pour water into the basin; if you can, lower the lights in your meeting space to create a more solemn mood. Have the youth pair off, and invite the pairs to come to the basins. Two by two, the partners will take turns washing each other's feet and drying them. Following the ritual, ask:

✝ How did the Scripture reading and this experience help you better understand Jesus' servanthood?

✝ How did you feel in the role of the foot washer?

You Will Need
- a Bible
- one wash cloth for each youth
- one towel for each youth
- a water basin
- a pitcher (optional)

Note: You may want to save the foot-washing ritual for Maundy Thursday. (See pages 46-47.)

Sacrifice: Palm Sunday

43

Note: If you have a large number of youth, use multiple wash basins.

Important: Instruct the youth not to put their feet in the water basin. Have the foot washer wet a clean wash cloth and use it to clean his or her partner's feet outside the basin. Do not rewet used wash cloths or place used wash cloths back into the basin.

You Will Need
- chairs

Defense Questions:
- What Christian practices do you faithfully observe?
- When have you reached out to someone in need?
- What have you done to deepen your relationship with God?

Prosecution Questions:
- When have you missed worship for no good reason?
- When have you failed to help someone in need?
- What decisions have you made without first going to God in prayer?

You Will Need
- a Bible

✝ How did you feel in the role of the recipient?

✝ How might this memorial help us better understand God's grace?

Say: "In first-century Judea, the act of washing feet was often reserved for a house servant. In a culture of pedestrians before the invention of sneakers, foot washing was dirty work. When Jesus washed feet, he demonstrated the love and humility required of all of God's followers."

Standing Trial

Arrange up to a dozen chairs into two rows along one wall to form a "jury box." Place two chairs on opposite ends of the jury box to create a "witness stand" and a defendant's chair. Set a "judge's bench" next to the witness stand.

Ask for one youth to be the defense attorney, another to be the prosecutor, and up to twelve to serve as jurors. You can play the role of the judge. Then ask any youth who are willing (including the jurors) to take the witness stand. The defense attorney should ask each witness questions that emphasize how the witness has stayed true to the faith. The prosecutor should challenge the witness to confess to aspects of his or her faith that need improvement. (For sample questions, see the margin.)

After all of the witnesses have been called, allow the jury to render a verdict. They should *not* say, "guilty" or "not guilty" but should answer questions such as, How faithful is our group? What do we do well? What needs improvement?

Closing Reflection

Select two youth to take turns reading aloud alternating verses from **Isaiah 50:4-9a** (God's servant is glorified for enduring suffering) as a closing reflection. The other youth should close their eyes during the reading. Following the Scripture, invite the youth to offer prayers either aloud or silently for themselves or for others.

Mission: Easter—Youth Programs & Ideas for Lent

Bible Study

Matthew 27:11-16

You will need Bibles, index cards, pens or pencils, and copies of the Bible Dictionary (pages 75–80). Optional: several Bible translations of the Bible, other Bible dictionaries, concordances, a large writing surface, and chalk or a marker.

Ask the youth to pair off and discuss the questions below with their partners. If you wish, write the questions on a large writing surface.

✛ What is the most difficult situation you have ever faced?
✛ When have you been falsely accused of doing something? How did you respond?
✛ What keeps you strong in times of adversity?

Gather the youth in a circle, and say: "Jesus' final hours were not pleasant. The twelve disciples abandoned him, Peter betrayed him, and he faced an agonizing and humiliating trial alone before suffering the torment of being whipped, beaten, and crucified. Yet Jesus remained faithful to God and endured these agonies so that we might know God's love more fully."

Divide the youth into groups of three or four. Ask a volunteer from each group to read aloud **Matthew 27:11-26** (Jesus' trial and crucifixion) while the others follow along. (If you have several translations of this text, have the groups read those translations.) Then have the groups discuss these questions (which you may write on a large writing surface):

✛ How does Jesus' trial compare with the trials held in America today?
✛ Why, do you think, did Jesus remain silent in the face of injustice?
✛ Why might the crowd have turned on Jesus?
✛ What does the trial of Jesus tell us about crowd mentality (thinking a certain way because everyone else seems to think that way)?
✛ When have you just followed the crowd?
✛ When has following the crowd caused you to hurt or ignore someone else?

Allow the groups time to discuss; then hand out index cards and pens or pencils. Gather the youth in a circle. Ask a youth to read aloud **Matthew 27:27-56**. (Option: Have other youth act out the roles of Jesus, Simon the Cyrene, the two bandits, the women at the foot of the cross, the soldiers, and the crowd as the text is read.)

Then have each youth write on his or her index card a question he or she would like to ask Jesus about his trial and crucifixion (such as, Why didn't you speak up? or Why didn't you save yourself?) When the youth have finished, collect the index cards. As a class, read and discuss the youths' questions one at a time. Discuss as many questions as time allows.

If you wish, ask the following questions in addition to or in lieu of the index-card activity:

✛ Would you say that Jesus chose death? Explain.
✛ What, do you think, is significant about the manner in which Jesus died?
✛ Why, do you think, were people mocking Jesus? Whom in today's world do we mock because of their goodness or sacrificial love?
✛ (Read aloud **Matthew 27:46**.) Why, do you think, did Jesus choose these verses from **Psalm 22** as his final words? (Read aloud **Psalm 22** and talk about how the psalm ends.)
✛ How do you think God was present in Jesus' death?
✛ How would you explain to another person the significance of Jesus' crucifixion?
✛ If someone asked you why a cross—an instrument of death and a symbol of pain and humiliation—is used to symbolize the Christian faith, what would you say?

If time permits, allow the youth to discuss any other questions or insights they might have. Then close in prayer, asking for strength, courage, and humility as you go out into the world to face trials that pale in comparison to what Jesus was up against.

Sacrifice: Palm Sunday

Maundy Thursday

Service: Maundy Thursday

Key Verse: "If you know these things, you are blessed if you do them" (**John 13:17**).

Old Testament: **Exodus 12:1-4, 11-14** (God institutes the Passover.)

New Testament: **John 13:1-17, 31b-35** (Jesus washes his disciples' feet.)

The Role of the Servant

Maundy Thursday, also known as Holy Thursday, commemorates Jesus' final night with his closest disciples. The word *Maundy* comes from the Latin word *mandatum*, which means "commandment" and refers to Jesus' commandment in **John 13:34**: "I give you a new commandment, that you love one another. Just as I have loved you, you also should love one another."

Maundy Thursday gives youth the opportunity to consider the role of service in the Christian life. On this day, Christians remember the Passover meal Jesus shared with his disciples on the night before his death. The three synoptic Gospels (Matthew, Mark, and Luke) preserve this story. John differs in that Jesus plays the role of a house servant, taking up a basin and towel and washing the disciples' feet.

Youth might find the tradition of foot washing odd, but the intimacy and gesture of this act of service has special significance in a world that often emphasizes individual gain. Rituals such as foot washing remind youth that we are called to set aside our needs and wants to serve others.

> **How can youth serve their communities?**

Create a Worship Experience

Use the suggestions on page 47 to create a Maundy Thursday worship experience for your youth. Consider incorporating one or more of the following ideas:

✝ Lead your youth in the foot-washing ritual found on pages 43–44.

✝ Have a Maundy Thursday Seder Meal. See the worship idea on page 71 for more information.

A Holy Thursday Prayer[†]

Before the service, write this prayer on a large writing surface or put it up on a PowerPoint® slide.

Gracious God,
   your Anointed One, on the night before he suffered,
instituted the sacrament of his body and blood.
Mercifully grant that we may receive it thankfully
   in remembrance of Jesus Christ our Lord,
   who in these holy mysteries
   gives us a pledge of eternal life. Amen.

[†] Reprinted from *The United Methodist Hymnal*, no. 283. Copyright © 1989 by The United Methodist Publishing House. Used by permission.

Mission: Easter—Youth Programs & Ideas for Lent

Agape Feast

Many early Christian communities had "agape* feasts." These simple meals of bread and water reminded them of God's love and the love found in the community. Over time, these feasts developed into what we know as Holy Communion, in which clergy preside over the table. But some church leaders, such as John Wesley, have encouraged churches to resurrect the love feast, since these meals do not necessitate the presence of a priest or pastor.

Gather the youth around a table or in a circle on the floor. Begin the meal by saying together a profession of faith, such as a creed from your congregation's hymnal or **Romans 6:3-4** (we are baptized into Christ's death). Then allow the teens to express any prayer concerns. Ask a youth to lead the group in prayer; close the prayer by saying together the Lord's Prayer.

After the prayer, pass the bread and instruct each youth to break off a small piece and serve it to the person to his or her right. Then pass the pitcher of water in the other direction and have each youth pour a cup of water for the person to his or her left.

When the youth have finished eating the bread and drinking the water, say: "People today express love in many ways: songs, letters, gifts, and so on. But these expressions of love do not necessarily help us when we try to understand God's love for the world. Agape love is radical, self-sacrificing love. In the agape feast, we serve one another and receive from one another as we grow as disciples of Jesus Christ."

You Will Need
- a loaf of bread to be shared by the group
- a pitcher of water
- a small cup for each person

* *Agape* (uh-GAH-pay) is one of three Greek words for love; it refers specifically to self-giving love—the love God has for us and expects us to have for others.

Make sure youth wash their hands before participating in the agape feast.

Dirty Feet, Clean Hearts

Ask a youth to read aloud **John 13:1-17, 31-35** (Jesus washes his disciples' feet). Then say: "Jesus offered many examples of service, but when he washed the disciples' feet he demonstrated the attitude and manner that we, his followers, should adopt. In Jesus' day, foot washing was a task performed by a servant when a guest entered the home. And back then, the average person's feet were filthy from walking barefoot or in sandals. By acting as a servant, Jesus showed his disciples that service should be a way of life." If time permits, discuss the questions printed in the margin.

You Will Need
- Bibles

Questions for Discussion
- Why might Peter have objected to Jesus washing Peter's feet?
- What unpleasant tasks might we be called to do for God? How can serving God be messy?

Go Forth, and Do Likewise

Ask the youth to brainstorm and list on a large writing surface projects your group could do in the coming year. These service projects could include working in a soup kitchen, sorting clothing at a thrift store, or helping the homebound with yard work. Encourage the youth to be creative. As a group, select three service projects to schedule and carry out. Close with the prayer printed on page 46.

You Will Need
- a large writing surface
- markers

Service: Maundy Thursday

Good Friday

Fear: Good Friday

Key Verse: "Let the Messiah, the King of Israel, come down from the cross now, so that we may see and believe" (**Mark 15:32a**).

Old Testament: Isaiah 52:13–53:12
(Isaiah describes God's suffering servant.)

New Testament: Mark 15:21-47
(Jesus dies on the cross.)

Why Is It Good?

Good Friday? What is so good about Jesus' death on the cross? Easter is the day that should be called "good." The Friday before Easter should be called "Black Friday" or "Bad Friday," but not Good Friday.

The origin of the name "Good Friday" is not certain. In fact, the Anglo-Saxons called the day "Long Friday," a name that Christians in Denmark still use. Still, most Christian calendars call the final Friday in Lent "Good Friday," so there must be something good about it.

Plenty about that Friday was anything but good. Crucifixion was an agonizing way to be put to death, and the pain of the cross was only outdone by the humiliation. The Roman government used crucifixion to make examples of persons they saw as a threat. By hanging radicals and revolutionaries on crosses, the rulers sent a message to the masses: "Watch yourself, or that victim will be you."

Though Jesus predicted his death and resurrection, the Gospels suggest that his closest followers weren't ready for what happened.

Their teacher's death shocked them, and they had doubts about his return. For those closest to Jesus, Good Friday was a day of fear and uncertainty.

Of course, Jesus suffered and died for a reason. By dying on that cross, Jesus sacrificed himself on our behalf. That bleak Friday afternoon that began the first Easter weekend initiated the saving act that would redeem all humanity. Good? Very good.

Regardless of their experiences, youth know suffering in one form or another and they know fear. Many know the feeling of hopelessness.

> **How can youth experience God's strength during difficult times?**

Good Friday proves that God is at work in even the most dire circumstances. A failed test may lead to a change in study habits that will help a youth throughout his or her academic career. A fight with a friend may force a youth to think critically about what it means to be in a relationship with someone. Even the loss of a loved one may inspire a youth to display that person's best qualities to others. Most importantly, because of Jesus' sacrifice on that first Good Friday, we know that God is actively working to heal all tragedies and redeem all humanity.

Create a Worship Experience

Use the suggestions on page 49 to create a Good Friday worship experience for your youth. Consider incorporating Follow the Stations of the Cross from the worship ideas (page 72).

Mission: Easter—Youth Programs & Ideas for Lent

Cross Words

Say: "You may find it odd that the day we recognize Jesus' death on a cross is referred to as 'Good Friday.' After all, we don't usually think of fear and suffering as 'good.' But the cross, that ancient instrument of death, also represents our redemption and reminds us that hope is never lost and that God can transform our despair and death into life-giving hope.

"The cross also reminds us that Jesus died for our sins. The least we can do in return is offer our lives to God." Instruct the youth to write on their strips of cloth one way in which they need God to transform their lives. Give the teens a few minutes to write, then have them offer up their needs to God by draping their strips of cloth on the cross.

You Will Need
- a cross about two feet tall
- one long strip of cloth for each youth
- markers

Suggestion: Designate an area of your meeting space that youth can use for individual prayer after they come to the cross.

At the Cross

Hand out the Bibles, and instruct the youth to silently read **Mark 15:21-47** (Jesus' death on the cross) and to think of questions or ideas that arise as they read. When they have finished reading, allow youth to voice any insights they gained from the Scripture and to ask any questions that arose. Give the teens plenty of time to discuss.

You Will Need
- Bibles

Meditations on the Cross

Display the pictures of crosses. Have the youth look at the crosses and consider what they mean and what they might have meant to the artist who created or photographed them. Encourage the teens to reflect on the following questions:

✝ Which cross reminds you most of the sacrifice of Jesus? Why?

✝ Which cross reminds you most fully of your role and calling as a disciple? Why?

Allow the youth to discuss their answers, and contribute your own answers. Say: "Though the cross has universal significance, it touches each person in a different way. From now on, when you see a cross, think about its redeeming power and what it means to you."

Hand out paper and pens or pencils, and ask each youth to write a short prayer based on **Mark 15:21-47**. This prayer could be a poem, thought, or reflection. Say a brief closing prayer, then allow the youth to read the prayers they have written.

To close, ask a youth to read aloud **Isaiah 52:13–53:12** (God's suffering servant).

You Will Need
- photographs, artists' representations, or Internet printouts of various crosses
- paper
- pens or pencils

Option: Hand out paper and markers or colored pencils, and have the youth create their own pictures of crosses. Encourage the teens to decorate the crosses in a way that represents the meaning of the cross as they understand it.

Fear: Good Friday

Easter Sunday

Hope: Easter Sunday

Key Verse: "If for this life only we have hoped in Christ, we are of all people most to be pitied. But in fact Christ has been raised from the dead, the first fruits of those who have died" (**1 Corinthians 15:19-20**).

Old Testament: **Ezekiel 36:24-28** (God vows to restore Israel.)

New Testament: **Matthew 28:1-10** (The women meet the risen Christ.)

Resurrection Hope

Living in the wealthiest country in the world, we now benefit from technological conveniences that previous generations could never have imagined. We have countless forms of entertainment, and we can be cured of diseases that were once fatal. But even now, we are surrounded by despair.

Every major American city is home to people who live on the streets, suffer from addictions, and don't know where their next meals will come from. Our media is saturated with put-downs; entertainers and politicians try to improve their profiles by insulting their colleagues and opponents. War and disease take millions of lives elsewhere in the world. And in the post-Oklahoma City, post-Columbine, post-September 11 America, everyone knows that we are never entirely safe.

While technology has enabled us to better communicate, heal, and learn, it has also enabled some to more effectively exploit, oppress, and destroy. Some nights, the evening news leaves viewers wondering, *Will we have a future in which to work, love, and pursue the joys of life? Will this future be secure, or will it contain threats, uncertainties, and destruction?*

Through the Internet and cable television, today's adolescents have become acutely aware of their vulnerabilities. And in a world connected by a global media and intercontinental travel, many youth have taken an interest in global issues such as war, epidemic diseases, oppression, famine, and poverty. Some young people are inevitably asking themselves, *Does our world have any hope? Where is God in the midst of all this human pain?*

Easter, Christ's victorious resurrection, is our ultimate hope. Resurrection out of death gave rise to the church: a people alive with the Holy Spirit, proclaiming hope in a hurting world. Resurrection is God's promise of life beyond life, of power that can overcome even death.

How can we find hope in Jesus' resurrection?

Today, on Easter Sunday, invite your youth to celebrate this hope, to live in it, and to be refreshed by the life-altering power of Christ, who redeems us and reminds us each day, "Take courage; I have conquered the world!" (**John 16:33b**).

50

Mission: Easter—Youth Programs & Ideas for Lent

Easter Sunday

Mission Plan

Activity	Supplies
Hopeful Happenings	• several front and local sections from daily newspapers
Resurrection Cards	• Bibles • construction paper • markers
Grave Matters	• Bibles
Testimony at the Tomb	• Bibles • copies of the Testimony at the Tomb handout (page 64)
Resurrection Songs	• hymnals or songbooks
Closing Prayer	• Bibles

Bible Study: Matthew 28:1–10

You will need Bibles, index cards, pens or pencils, and copies of the Bible Dictionary (pages 75–80) Optional: other Bible dictionaries, concordances, atlases, a large writing surface, and chalk or a marker.

You Will Need
- several front and local sections from daily newspapers

Hopeful Happenings

As the youth arrive, hand each of them a section of the newspaper. When most of the youth have arrived, say: "So often we are bombarded with bad news in our communities, our schools, and our world. But if we look closely enough, we can see glimmers of hope, which God offers us." Instruct the teens to read through their newspaper sections and look for one story that demonstrates hope in a hurting world.

Allow the youth about five minutes to skim the papers for an appropriate story. Then ask the youth to summarize aloud the stories they have selected. (If you have a large group, divide the youth into smaller groups and have the youth in each group summarize its stories.) Then ask:

✞ What evidence of God's presence can you see in today's world?

✞ As Christians, how is our notion of hope connected to the resurrection of Jesus Christ?

Say: "Christianity began on Easter. When Jesus overcame death, God radically demonstrated the promise of life beyond life and gave us hope for all time."

You Will Need
- Bibles
- construction paper
- markers

Suggested Verses
- **Matthew 28:5-6**
- **John 16:33**
- **Titus 3:6-7**
- **Hebrews 10:23**

Resurrection Cards

Distribute the construction paper and markers, and instruct the youth to create Easter cards for persons in their congregation or community or elsewhere who are somehow in need of hope and God's healing touch. Remind the teens to include in their cards the message of Easter: Christ is alive, and God is with us. Encourage the teens to add their personal artistic touches and to include appropriate Bible verses. (See the suggestions in the margin.)

You Will Need
- Bibles

Grave Matters

Ask a volunteer to read aloud **Matthew 28:1-10** (Christ's resurrection). Then say: "By Jewish custom, a body was ritually prepared for burial using spices such as myrrh. Women traditionally performed this unpleasant task, but they could not prepare Jesus' body Friday evening because the Jewish sabbath begins Friday at sunset. So the women went to Jesus' tomb on the Sunday morning following the to prepare his body." Ask, "Where were the men, especially the twelve disciples?"

If the youth do not offer the correct response, say: "The men had fled. We learn from other Gospel accounts that the men initially refused to believe the women's story about the empty tomb.

52

Mission: Easter—Youth Programs & Ideas for Lent

According to the customs of the time, it took the testimony of two women to count as a valid witness. (Men could be credible witnesses by themselves.) And a woman's testimony was given little credence, especially if a man contradicted what a woman said.* Given the context, the fact that women were the first evangelists is particularly noteworthy." Ask:

✟ How do you envision the scene of the women at the tomb?

✟ What do you think the tomb was like?

Say: "Jesus was likely buried in a family crypt, in which people were commonly buried at that time. This practice is what the Bible refers to when it calls death 'sleeping with one's fathers.' The crypts—sometimes caves covered with stones or one giant rolling stone—were opened only when another member of the family died.† Nonetheless, when the angel rolled back the stone the tomb was already empty; Jesus' body had vanished."

*See **Mark 16:9-11; Luke 24:10-11,** and **Luke 24:22-24.**

† See **John 11:38-41.**

Testimony at the Tomb

Distribute Testimony at the Tomb handout on page 64. With the help of your youth, assign the various roles for the dramatic reading. (If you are working with a small number of youth, ask some youth to assume more than one role.) This dramatic reading features questions about the Resurrection that people today might ask, with answers presented by the eyewitnesses at the tomb. If time permits, ask for volunteers to read each of the Scripture references in italics. Following the reading, ask the youth what insights about Christ's resurrection they have gained.

You Will Need
- Bibles
- copies of the Testimony at the Tomb handout (page 64)

Resurrection Songs

Hand out the hymnals or songbooks, and ask youth to read the lyrics of Resurrection-themed hymns. (See the margin for examples.) Ask:

✟ What do the hymn writers say about Christ's resurrection?

✟ What themes or symbols do the writers use in these hymns?

Sing one or two of the hymns. If you have access to a piano or organ and one or more of your youth play, allow them to accompany.

You Will Need
- hymnals or songbooks

Examples
- "Christ the Lord Is Risen Today," by Charles Wesley
- "The Day of Resurrection," by John of Damascus
- "He Lives," by Alfred Ackley
- "He Rose," African American spiritual

Closing Prayer

Gather the youth in a circle, and invite them to mention any prayer concerns or joys they may have. Allow for a brief moment of silent prayer to lift up spoken and unspoken requests. Close by having a youth read aloud **Philippians 2:5-11**. This passage, one of the oldest Christian hymns, is an excellent affirmation of the Easter faith.

You Will Need
- a Bible

Hope: Easter Sunday

Bible Study

Matthew 28:1-10

You Will Need *Bibles, index cards, pens or pencils, and copies of the Bible Dictionary (pages 76–80). Optional: other Bible dictionaries, concordances, Bible atlases, a markerboard or large sheet of paper, markers.*

Ask a youth to read aloud **Matthew 28:1-10** (Christ's resurrection) while the others follow along. Then divide the youth into four groups and distribute any concordances, Bible dictionaries, or other reference materials equally among the groups. Assign each group one of the terms below, and instruct the groups to find the information necessary to answer the questions related to their terms. (If you have a large number of youth, divide the youth into eight groups and assign each term to two groups. If you have a small number of youth, assign two terms to each group or one term to each youth.)

Sabbath
✞ How was the Jewish sabbath observed in Jesus' day?

✞ What rituals and cautions were observed on the sabbath?

Mary Magdalene
✞ Who was Mary, and where was she from?
✞ How was Mary significant among Jesus' disciples?

Tomb, Sepulchre, and Jewish Burial
✞ What rituals and practices were associated with Jewish burial in Jesus' time?

✞ What was a first-century Jewish tomb like?

Galilee
✞ Where was Galilee? What was its significance for Jesus and his disciples? Why, do you think, Jesus appeared to his disciples in Galilee?

✞ Where was Galilee in relation to Judea (specifically Jerusalem)? How did Galilee differ from Judea?

Give the groups plenty of time to research and answer the questions; then ask for a representative from each group to summarize for the others what the group has learned.

Divide youth into groups of two or three (if your groups are not already that small). Ask the groups to discuss the questions below, which you might write on a markerboard or large sheet of paper:

✞ What would be your first inclination if a friend were to tell you she had seen a dead person come back to life? Why might you have difficulty believing this account?

✞ What fears do you associate with death?

✞ Why, do you think, do people have difficulty talking about death?

Gather the youth into a circle, and ask a youth to read aloud **Matthew 28:1-10** again. Then ask:

✞ What do you think the women expected to find at the tomb?

✞ How do you envision Mary Magdalene's reaction to discovering the tomb's vacancy?

✞ Why is it significant that Jesus sent the women to tell the disciples in Galilee that he had risen?

✞ Where might the disciples have expected to find Jesus?

✞ What questions do you have that Matthew's account of the story does not address?

Invite a volunteer to read aloud **1 Corinthians 15:35-44** (the Resurrection body). Then ask:

✞ How does this passage describe resurrection? What does Paul have to say about our bodies?

✞ How does Paul's description enhance your faith?

Ask a youth to say a prayer of eternal hope amid a world of temporary pain and uncertainty.

Mission: Easter—Youth Programs & Ideas for Lent

Tempting Roleplays

One youth will roleplay each of the characters below, either by reading the description aloud or by creatively developing the character based on the given information. After each character is presented, the youth on the outside of the circle may offer advice to help the character with his or her problems.

Quentin or Kenna: My name is [Quentin or Kenna], and lately I've been struggling. Most of my friends spend their Friday and Saturday nights experimenting with drugs, and I'm feeling left out. So far, I've turned them down every time they've offered me something; but they seem to be having so much fun. I feel so bored—and so boring—just standing there while everyone else is high. I know about the consequences of taking drugs, but sometimes I really want to join in. I don't want to quit hanging out with my friends, but I'm not sure I can hold out much longer when they offer me drugs. What should I do?

Dora or Donny: My name is [Dora or Donny], and I've been dating [Jimmy or Jamie] for two years. The two of us are getting serious, and sometimes we've been going a little too far when we're alone. [Jimmy or Jamie] insists that if we love each other it's OK to have some type of sex. But I'm not sure. I enjoy our time alone, and I have sexual desires of my own; but I'm not sure that I'm ready and I'm worried about what might happen. What should I do?

Tammy or Tim: My name is [Tammy or Tim]. Last week a group of my so-called friends completely dissed me at a party. I'm ticked off and would love to get back at them. I'm thinking about taking some things from Eric's locker, sabotaging one of Josephina's tests, and maybe even spreading a few lies about Leslie. I can't stand thinking about them hanging out without me, and revenge would be so sweet. But I'm not sure that getting back at them is the best way to handle the situation. What should I do?

© 2005 Abingdon Press. Permission is granted to reproduce this page for use with
Mission: Easter—Youth Programs & Ideas for Lent. All rights reserved.

55

Lead Us Not Into Temptation

Reflect on each of the following questions:

✗ What is the difference between temptation and sin?

✗ What do we mean when we pray in the Lord's prayer, "Lead us not into temptation"?

✗ How are people your age "led into temptation"?

Prayerfully consider your life and some of the temptations you are facing. Then answer the following questions:

✗ What three temptations are most difficult for people your age to overcome?

  1.

  2.

  3.

✗ What three temptations do you struggle with the most?

  1.

  2.

  3.

✗ What do you need from God right now to better deal with temptation?

✗ Where in your life do you need God's healing and forgiveness?

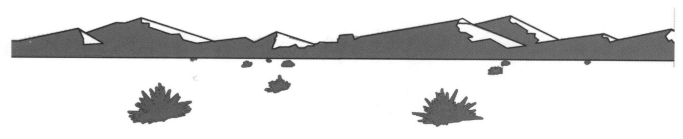

Giving It Up for Lent

As far back as the fourth century A.D., Christians have considered the forty days leading up to Easter as a time of sacrifice, which has meant fasting. Some Christians have observed this fast by simply abstaining from meats other than fish, while others have eaten only dry bread. Some have avoided certain foods for the duration of Lent, while others have gone hours or days without eating anything before specified times. Today, members of some Christian traditions give up certain foods or habits during the Lenten season. Though Christians have practiced this fast in many different ways throughout the years, sacrificing something for Lent has been an important part of Christian tradition throughout the centuries.

By giving up something, we inevitably make room for something else. By sacrificing certain foods, habits, or comforts, we save time, money, or energy that we could devote to other purposes. This Lent, make a commitment not only to give up something—whether chocolate, putting people down, or biting your nails—but also to pick up something else that involves serving God and others.

- Below or on the back of this page, list some possible sacrifices you could make this Lenten season. Then circle one sacrifice that you want to commit to for the next six weeks.

- Now list one way you can use the time, money, or energy you will save by giving up something for Lent to serve God or others.

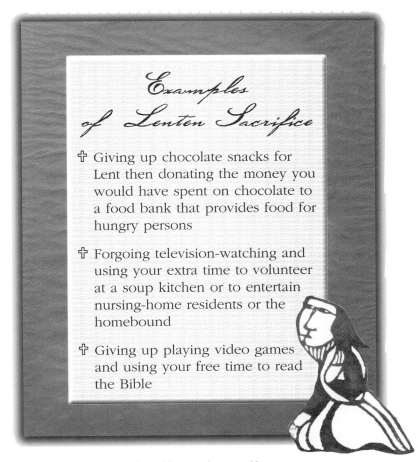

Examples of Lenten Sacrifice

✝ Giving up chocolate snacks for Lent then donating the money you would have spent on chocolate to a food bank that provides food for hungry persons

✝ Forgoing television-watching and using your extra time to volunteer at a soup kitchen or to entertain nursing-home residents or the homebound

✝ Giving up playing video games and using your free time to read the Bible

© 2005 Abingdon Press. Permission is granted to reproduce this page for use with MISSION: EASTER—YOUTH PROGRAMS & IDEAS FOR LENT. All rights reserved.

Circles of Influence

Read **Hebrews 12:1**. Then in this circle, list five people who have influenced your faith:

Read **Romans 12:1-2**. Then in this circle, list five people whom you believe you influence in a positive way:

Complete the following sentences:

☺ I am thankful for _____ for helping me _____.

☺ I dedicate myself to helping _____.

☺ I believe I can sacrifice the most for Christ by _____.

☺ The best thing I can do for God this week is _____.

© 2005 Abingdon Press. Permission is granted to reproduce this page for use with
MISSION: EASTER—YOUTH PROGRAMS & IDEAS FOR LENT. All rights reserved.

Coming Events

Read **Luke 13:6-9**. Think about how long it takes for a tree to grow. Consider everything a tree needs to reach maturity, stand tall against the elements, and bear fruit. Now consider your life and the journey you are on. Some goals in your life may take a long time to achieve, but you can achieve them only by being faithful to those goals and striving with God to make them a reality.

List two of your long-term goals, such as becoming a doctor, owning a home, or landing a record deal. Beneath each long-term goal, list two short-term goals that will help you reach your long-term goal, such as keeping your grades up, putting a certain amount of money into savings, or getting a band together.

1.
   a.
   b.
2.
   a.
   b.

Now consider what you will need to achieve those goals. What will you need from God? from others? from yourself?

Now list two long-term spiritual goals you have for you life, such as the ability to put God ahead of everything else or expressing your faith in a way that draws people to Christ. Beneath each long-term goal, list two short-term goals that will help you reach your long-term goal, such as starting a daily devotional practice or committing to regular acts of service.

1.
   a.
   b.
2.
   a.
   b.

© 2005 Abingdon Press. Permission is granted to reproduce this page for use with MISSION: EASTER—YOUTH PROGRAMS & IDEAS FOR LENT. All rights reserved.

What? ...God Use Me?

Take a few minutes to read the Bible passages on this page; then complete each sentence.

Now there are varieties of gifts, but the same Spirit; and there are varieties of services, but the same Lord; and there are varieties of activities, but it is the same God who activates all them in everyone.
—1 Corinthians 12:4-6

I believe that my strengths are _____.

Likewise, the Spirit helps us in our weakness.
—Romans 8:26a

I believe that my weaknesses are _____.

Let us run with perseverance the race that is set before us.
—Hebrews 12:1b

My passions (what I truly enjoy doing) are

_____

_____.

Do not neglect to do good and to share what you have, for such sacrifices are pleasing to God.
—Hebrews 13:16

Some acts of service that I can perform for others are _____

_____

_____.

We know that all things work together for good for those who love God, who are called according to his purpose.
—Romans 8:28

With God's help, I believe that I can become

_____

_____

_____.

Heart Prayer

Leader: God, you have searched us and found us.

Youth: Know my heart, O God.

Leader: You have given each of us gifts of your Spirit.

Youth: Know my heart, O God.

Leader: You have called us back from the far country.

Youth: Know my heart, O God.

Leader: You call us to be your children and to serve the weak and the needy.

Youth: Know my heart, O God.

All: For you are a great God and greatly to be praised.

© 2005 Abingdon Press. Permission is granted to reproduce this page for use with
MISSION: EASTER—YOUTH PROGRAMS & IDEAS FOR LENT. All rights reserved.

God Stuff

Works of Justice and Mercy

Let justice roll down like waters, and righteousness like an everflowing stream.
—Amos 5:24

Works of justice and mercy involve our awareness of life's inequalities, injustices, and social needs. We can see the church's involvement in these works of God today through homeless shelters, soup kitchens, efforts to bring about more just labor laws, concern for people with AIDS, and the many individual acts offered out of love for others.

How and in what situations might you demonstrate your love for others by showing mercy?

_____

_____

_____

_____

_____

_____

How and in what situations should our congregation be involved in matters of peace and justice?

_____

_____

_____

_____

_____

_____

Works of Prayer and Contemplation

My soul thirsts for God, for the living God.
—Psalm 42:2a

Both as individuals and as a church, Christians have always used prayer, silence, study, contemplation, and openness to the Spirit to grow spiritually, deepen their faith, and discern God's direction.

How can you grow in your prayer life and your willingness to seek God's direction?

_____

_____

_____

_____

_____

_____

_____

_____

How might we as a congregation deepen our awareness of God?

_____

_____

_____

_____

_____

_____

© 2005 Abingdon Press. Permission is granted to reproduce this page for use with
MISSION: EASTER—YOUTH PROGRAMS & IDEAS FOR LENT. All rights reserved.

God Stuff, Continued

Works of Evangelism

Jesus said to her, "I am the resurrection and the life. Those who believe in me, even though they die, will live, and everyone who lives and believes in me will never die."

—John 11:25-26a

Christians have a concern for those who do not know Christ or feel his love. The church grows by reaching out to those who are hurting, lost, or in need of God's redemption.

How can you use your voice, hands, or talents to invite others to know God's love?

_____

_____

_____

_____

_____

_____

How might our church reach out more effectively to our community?

_____

_____

_____

_____

_____

Works of Virtue

Train yourself in godliness, for, while physical training is of some value, godliness is valuable in every way, holding promise for both the present life and the life to come.

—1 Timothy 4:7b-8

The many virtues of the Christian life include joy, peace, helpfulness, honesty, integrity, and self-control. Christians strive to improve their lives through self-discipline and by turning their attentions and goals toward God each day.

How might you grow in your spiritual disciplines?

_____

_____

_____

_____

_____

_____

How might our church help people live more virtuous lives?

_____

_____

_____

_____

_____

Stations of the Trial

Station One: Jesus Stands Before Pilate, the Roman Prefect **(Matthew 27:11-14)**

✝ Why are we always so quick to defend ourselves, Lord, when you endured the shame of false accusations calmly and patiently?

Station Two: Pilate Offers Barabbas or Jesus **(Matthew 27:15-17)**

✝ Why do we frequently offer others and ourselves "quick fixes" instead of Jesus?

Station Three: Pilate Sits in Judgment **(Matthew 27:19-20)**

✝ Why do we often sit in judgment instead of compassion? in ridicule instead of helpfulness?

Station Four: The People Reject Jesus **(Matthew 27:21-23)**

✝ How do we reject you, Lord, through what we say, demand, or do?

Station Five: Pilate Condemns Jesus to Die **(Matthew 27:24-26)**

✝ How do we condemn you, Lord, through anger, apathy, or refusing to take a stand for you?

Litany of Love

Jesus: I came among you as a shepherd, savior, and friend.

People: But we treated you as a liar, a fraud, and an outcast.

Jesus: I came among you to heal and make new.

People: But we left you to die and preferred to keep things as they were.

Jesus: I came among you in spirit and in truth.

People: But we preferred our own way and the pathways of deceit.

Jesus: I came among you with love, joy, and peace.

People: But we preferred the old ways of hatred, prejudice, and war. Forgive us, Lord! Help us to walk in your narrow way, and free us to abandon those paths that lead only to death, destruction, and despair. Give us your spirit, your peace, and your love, that we may be saved in the time of trial.

© 2005 Abingdon Press. Permission is granted to reproduce this page for use with
MISSION: EASTER—YOUTH PROGRAMS & IDEAS FOR LENT. All rights reserved.

Testimony at the Tomb

The eight disciples in this script represent teenagers today who are struggling with their faith.

Mary Magdalene: I was the first to see the empty tomb, and I know my Lord is alive. (*Mark 16:9*)

Disciple 1: Why should I believe that Jesus is alive when my human experience tells me that death is the end?

Joanna: God raised Jesus from the dead as a proclamation God's promise of eternal life in Christ. (*Luke 24:10*)

Disciple 2: But how can I believe in someone I haven't seen?

Cleopas: I didn't know Jesus when I saw him either. But he made himself known to me when he broke the bread. (*Luke 24:30-31*)

Disciple 3: But I haven't seen Jesus. How can I know that this testimony holds water?

Emmaus Disciple: Jesus was present to us when we discussed the Scriptures, and our hearts burned with his presence. (*Luke 24:32*)

James: I didn't recognize Jesus when he came to us at the Sea of Galilee. (*John 21:4*)

Peter: And I didn't see Jesus until he spoke my name! (*John 21:7-8*)

Disciple 4: But I have doubts about Jesus being alive! Does that mean I'm not a person of faith?

Thomas: I had doubts too—and I was there! I once told my friends that I would not believe, but Jesus later told me that those who believe without seeing are truly blessed. (*John 20:24-29*)

Disciple 5: Hold up a minute! Are you saying that even the first disciples doubted what they were seeing?

John: Some of us doubted when we saw Jesus on the mountain in Galilee. Others doubted what others professed to see. After all, it is not easy to believe that Jesus could be alive as our redeemer and friend. It's almost too good to be true! (*Matthew 28:17; Mark 16:11, 13*)

Disciple 6: But I want proof!

Hebrews Writer: People also wanted proof when Jesus healed the sick and announced the kingdom. But Jesus said no proof would be given. Faith is the conviction of things not seen. (*Hebrews 11:1-2*)

Disciple 7: I don't get this Resurrection business. How can God raise a body that's turned into dust and ashes?

Paul: Hold on! Don't limit God's power. You're right, we would be foolish to believe that our present earthly bodies can inherit a new life with God. Our present bodies will decay, but God will raise us to inherit a heavenly body fit for eternal life. (*1 Corinthians 15:35-44*)

Disciple 8: Well, faith is tough enough to come by these days. But is a little faith good enough for God?

Jesus: Listen carefully. Even if you have a faith that is as small as a mustard seed, nothing will be impossible for you! Trust in me. Don't be afraid. I am alive forever! (*Matthew 17:20-21; 28:20*)

All: I believe that you died and that you were raised from death on the third day. You are alive forever, and you are my redeemer and friend.

© 2005 Abingdon Press. Permission is granted to reproduce this page for use with MISSION: EASTER—YOUTH PROGRAMS & IDEAS FOR LENT. All rights reserved.

Temptation Survivor*

Based on Matthew 4:1-11 and Luke 4:1-13

CHARACTERS
Todd, *host of* Temptation Survivor
Debbie, *contestant on* Temptation Survivor
Hank the Tank, *contestant on* Temptation Survivor

Todd: It's been a rough week for Debbie on *Temptation Survivor*. Debbie and Hank the Tank are the remaining members of the Tooka Looka Tribe. Can they stay in the game, or will they be eliminated by this week's challenge?

Debbie: Any luck? I sure hope you caught some fish.

Hank: Sorry, totally. Using your earring as a fishhook and lure seemed like a wicked idea.

Debbie: If you didn't catch anything, at least give me back the earring. I may be starving, but I can at least look hip when we show up for Tribal Council.

Hank: Sorry, totally.

Debbie: What do you mean, "Sorry, totally?"

Hank: Gone, like totally gone. Some fish swallowed it. Wicked fish.

Debbie: Great! I don't think I can survive another day on slugs and seaweed. Have any other "wicked ideas"?

Notes

*Written by Beth Miller. Copyright © 2004 by Helen Elizabeth Miller. All rights reserved. Used by permission.

Notes

Hank: Yeah. Like, it would be totally wicked to steal the homemade bread from the Bongo Bongo Tribe.

Debbie: The Bongo Bongo Tribe has bread? Get out of here! I'd die for bread.

Hank: Yeah. When I climbed the summit of the island this morning, I saw a fishing boat delivering loaves of bread.

Debbie: Loaves? Get out of here! You mean they not only have homemade bread but they also have loaves and loaves?

Hank: Totally. With butter and jam. They threw the leftovers to the fish. Wicked—huh?

Debbie: So how did you get close enough to see the butter and jam?

Hank: I snuck through the jungle. I was close enough I could have bagged two or three loaves. They would never have missed them. Wicked—totally.

Debbie: So why didn't you? You dim-witted oaf. I'm starving. Besides, you lost my earring; you owe me something.

Hank: Wicked—totally.

Debbie: Will you please stop all this "wicked—totally" jargon?!

Hank: No, 'cause what you're asking is "wicked—totally." Stealing is wrong. Have some more seaweed.

Debbie: Uck. I'll tell you what's wicked—this seaweed is wicked.

Hank: Well, a person doesn't live by bread alone.

Todd: Hank the Tank saved the day. So Debbie and Hank remain in the game. Tune in next week when Hank takes Debbie to the pinnacle of the island and she can choose to take over any tribe she sees.

© 2005 Abingdon Press. Permission is granted to reproduce this page for use with
Mission: Easter—Youth Programs & Ideas for Lent. All rights reserved.

Trading Places*

CHARACTERS

Shelley, *host of* Trading Places
Heather, *teenage participant on the show*

Shelley: Welcome to *Trading Places*, where every Friday American teens get to choose whether to trade places with someone else. Welcome, Heather.

Heather: This is *so* exciting. I'm a really big fan. I watch your show every week.

Shelley: Heather, this has to be difficult for you. As far as life as a high school senior goes, you seem to have it made.

Heather: You're right. I expected to be Homecoming Queen and to be voted "Most Likely to Succeed"; but when the Rhodes Scholarship came through and Dad threw in the BMW, it just seemed like life couldn't get any better.

Shelley: Then you won *American Idolatry* and *Who Wants to Be a Billionaire*.

Heather: You forgot to mention that I also won *The Appurtenance*.

Shelley: Heather, I have to say it sounds like you have it all. Whom could you possibly want to trade lives with?

Heather: God.

Shelley: God?

Heather: Yeah. God Almighty.

Shelley: God, who was incarnate in Jesus Christ?

Heather: Exactly.

Notes

Suggestion: Adapt the script by using your own TV reality show parodies.

appurtenance (uh-PUR-tents): a right or privilege that comes with ownership of property

*Written by Beth Miller. Copyright © 2004 by Helen Elizabeth Miller. All rights reserved. Used by permission.

© 2005 Abingdon Press. Permission is granted to reproduce this page for use with
MISSION: EASTER—YOUTH PROGRAMS & IDEAS FOR LENT. All rights reserved.

Notes

Shelley: Do you want to reconsider?

Heather: Definitely not. I want to have all of the power. I want to know everything. I want people to worship me and me alone.

Shelley: Do you know what you're asking?

Heather: Sure. I want to trade lives with Jesus Christ—God as a human being.

Shelley: You do realize that this is Good Friday?

Heather: Sure, it's a good Friday; it's a great Friday as far as I'm concerned.

Shelley: OK. Well, let's go. Our fabulous crew has arranged for Heather to trade lives with Jesus Christ on Good Friday.

Heather: Wow, I love the setting. Pilate has some nice digs. This is great. Pilate is the man in charge—the Roman prefect, the guy with power and influence. You brought me to the right place.

Shelley: This is just the first place you will be going. Next, you will go to Herod and then back here. At that point Pilate will take you out on the balcony and the crowd will vote.

Heather: Nothing to worry about. We're talking about a crowd that welcomed Jesus into Jerusalem last Sunday waving palm branches, laying their coats in the road, and shouting, "Hosanna! Blessed is he who comes in the name of the Lord!" Right?

Shelley: You've got that part of the story right; but this is Holy Week, remember?

Heather: No problem. Holy Week—Easter, chocolate bunnies, lilies, new clothes with shoes to match, the Hallelujah chorus, and me triumphant for all time. . . . But, Shelley, I do have a bit of a problem with the costume people.

© 2005 Abingdon Press. Permission is granted to reproduce this page for use with
MISSION: EASTER—YOUTH PROGRAMS & IDEAS FOR LENT. All rights reserved.

Shelley: Heather, you've requested Jesus Christ on Good Friday, right?

Heather: Right. But Jesus Christ is God; so why do I have to wear this crown of thorns? It's real! And it really hurts. I think the Son of God deserves something at least as nice as my Homecoming crown—you know, gold with authentic gems.

Shelley: The script calls for a crown of thorns.

Heather: Well, this won't do. I'm not going out into a courtyard full of fans wearing this. They're going to be voting on my future. I'm a real expert on winning—just look at my record. I can tell you that a crown of thorns won't make me a winner.

Shelley: The crew works hard to make this historically accurate.

Heather: Well, then where are my twelve disciples? Aren't they my personal fan club? I thought they followed me everywhere.

Shelley: Sorry. They ditched you after the party in the upper room last night.

Heather: And who wrote this script for Christ's life? "Blessed are the meek"? "Pray for those who persecute you"? "The last will be first and the first last"? There's a story about a father who actually throws a party when his rebellious punk of a son comes home after wasting all of his money; there's another one where people work all day in a vineyard and get paid the same as the losers who show up at the last hour. Where's the fairness in that? Whoever wrote this script must have been in the sun too long or something, because their cheese is sliding off their cracker. Who came up with this, anyway?

See
- Matthew 5:5
- Matthew 5:44b
- Mark 10:31
- Luke 15:11-32
- Matthew 20:1-16

Shelley: Jesus Christ.

Notes

See
- Matthew 26:39b
- Luke 23:34
- Mark 15:34b
- John 19:30a

See John 14:6.

Heather: Exactly. And I have real trouble with these lines: "Not my will but yours be done"; "Father, forgive them for they know not what they are doing"; "My God, why have you forsaken me"; "It is finished." Shelley, I just can't imagine myself saying any of these lines.

Shelley: I can't either. Heather, you do know the part about the cross, don't you?

Heather: Sure. See this gold cross necklace? I even have earrings to match.

Shelley: Heather, you have to carry the cross, be crucified, and die.

Heather: No way.

Shelley: Way, truth, and life.

Heather: Get out of here! I mean, get me out of here! This is a joke, right? I don't need to be trading places. This is an outrage! I can't do this.

Shelley: Jesus is willing to trade places; after all, that's what he did the first time.

Heather: Wow. I'm so relieved.

Shelley: That's fine; seems Jesus found your life a little unsatisfactory.

© 2005 Abingdon Press. Permission is granted to reproduce this page for use with MISSION: EASTER—YOUTH PROGRAMS & IDEAS FOR LENT. All rights reserved.

Worship Ideas

Have a Maundy Thursday Seder Meal [1]

Many Christian traditions have begun participating in Seder meals during Lent and some specifically on Maundy Thursday. By connecting the history of our faith to the death and Resurrection of our Savior, we linger on the promise that God has a plan for us from the beginning. Seder meals include a variety of different foods, smells, drinks, and a ceremonial hand-washing service—talk about multisensory! The meal is conducted with a precise order of service as to how things are supposed to occur. In fact, the word *Seder* means "order" and refers to the sequence in which different elements of the meal happen.

For detailed instructions for hosting a Seder meal, visit *www.cresourcei.org/haggadah.html.*

Host an Agape Feast [2]

The love (*agape*) feast is a meal of Christian fellowship that mirrors the meals Jesus shared with his disciples and others throughout his ministry. Fellowship and community are celebrated around the theme of a meal.

The love feast should not be confused with Communion, but it is similar in some ways. Hold your love feast around a common table with a full banquet of finger foods in various baskets. Have a common cup or pitcher of juice, lemonade, tea, or other beverage. Distribute the food by passing around the baskets and the pitcher.

While the food is being passed, have volunteers read aloud Scripture passages about meals or banquets (for instance, **Luke 9:12-17**, Jesus feeds the multitudes; **Luke 14:16-24**, the parable of the great dinner; or **John 6:25-35**, Jesus is the bread of life). Sing hymns or praise songs and share testimonies. When everyone has been served, have a time of community prayers. Pray for the needs of your group, the needs of your community, your world, and so on. Open the prayer so that everyone gets a chance to pray. Use this time to celebrate and unify the group.

Touch the Cross [3]

Sometime during Lent, gather around a wooden cross as you tell the story of the Crucifixion. Have a prayer time that gives youth a chance to feel the cross as they pray. If you incorporate this idea for an indoor service, lean the cross against the altar table and drape colored cloth over it. Surround the cross with tea light candles as the only light in the room.

Often the cross in the worship space is far removed from the congregation. For this worship experience, allow the youth to be as close to the cross as possible to give them an added sense of awe in prayer.

Wash One Another's Feet [4]

In the time of the Scripture writers, people walked on foot to get where they were going. They literally carried their burdens on their feet. Recall the many references to washing feet in Scripture, from Genesis to the New Testament. This act symbolized servanthood, hospitality, and friendship. Take time as a community to wash one another's feet and reflect on any one of the passages in the Bible that speak of the ritual.

A variation on this act is the giving of back rubs. Our feet do not necessarily carry our stresses and burdens these days; instead we feel stress in the back and neck areas. Liken the practice of foot washing to caring for one another by rubbing the shoulders of a friend.

Use a Labyrinth [5]

This ancient practice is a contemplative exercise that involves walking through a maze in order to center on Christ. A labyrinth outlined on the floor presents a vivid image that can enhance the environment of worship. Even if a person doesn't walk through the labyrinth, it is a valuable tool for contemplation. A simple element like masking tape on carpet can create the desired effect. If meeting outside, use sand, chalk, bricks, or small stones. If possible, involve members of the community in creating the labyrinth. This activity is especially appropriate during special seasons such as Lent or Advent. The labyrinth is intended to be a place where one focuses on prayer. As the participants walk the maze-like pattern, they should allow themselves to focus solely on listening for God's still small voice. Once the worshipers have made it to the center of the labyrinth, they are to sit quietly and listen for what God might be saying through the Scripture. As each person exits the circle, he or she is to focus on what God is calling him or her to do in the world and how to go about living differently.

Follow the Stations of the Cross [6]

Set up fourteen small wooden crosses in your worship space or on your church yard. Make a handout with the following information and let your youth walk to each cross to pray and meditate at their own pace.

1. Jesus goes before Pilate **(Matthew 27:11-31)**. Pray that others would know that you are a Christian by your life.

2. Jesus takes up his cross **(John 19:17)**. Pray that you would have the courage to take up your cross and follow Jesus.

3. Jesus falls. Pray that you would walk tall and not stumble in your faith.

4. Jesus seeks care for his mother **(John 19:25-27)**. Pray for your family.

5. Simon carries Jesus' cross **(Mark 15:21)**. Pray for the strength to support others.

6. Jesus' face is wiped. Pray for the courage to be kind.

7. Jesus falls again. Pray for those who cause you to stumble.

8. Women weep for Jesus **(Luke 23:27)**. Pray for those who may be grieving.

9. Jesus falls again. Pray for power to stand against injustice.

10. Jesus' clothes are stripped **(John 19:23-25)**. Pray for those who have been violated in this world.

11. Jesus is nailed to the cross **(Mark 15:37)**. Praise Christ for taking your place.

12. Jesus dies **(Mark 15:37)**. Pray for the hope that only God can give.

13. Jesus is taken off the cross **(Luke 23:50-53)**. Pray for the courage to live for Christ.

14. Jesus is buried **(John 19:38)**. Pray that you would live your faith actively and abundantly in the world.

Visit the Wilderness [7]

During Lent, take the participants to a nearby state park and have your worship experience in the middle of the forest and focus on "being in the wilderness" of our lives.

[1] Reprinted from *Worship Feast Ideas: 100 Awesome Ideas for Postmodern Youth*, page 65. Copyright © 2003 by Abingdon Press. Used by permission.
[2] *Worship Feast Ideas*, p. 68.
[3] *Worship Feast Ideas*, p. 88.
[4] *Worship Feast Ideas*, p. 92.
[5] *Worship Feast Ideas*, p. 96.
[6] *Worship Feast Ideas*, pp. 106–107.
[7] *Worship Feast Ideas*, p. 104.

For more information on *Worship Feast Ideas* and the rest of the *Worship Feast* line, visit *www.ilead youth.com/catalog.asp?CatalogType=4.*

Lenten Retreat Plan

Getting Away for Lent

The Lenten season is traditionally a time when many Christians retreat together to spend extended time in prayer, study, and community building. The retreat schedule below is one way to combine the sessions and activities from this book into a weekend experience that youth would enjoy.

Friday Evening

7:00 Arrive at the retreat location and get acquainted with one another.

7:30 Do activities and rituals selected from the Ash Wednesday program (pages 8–9).

8:15 Take a break and have snacks.

9:15 Do activities selected from the First Sunday of Lent program (pages 10–15).

10:15 Play games, sing songs, or allow for free time before lights out.

Saturday Morning

8:00 Eat breakfast.

9:00 Start the day with fun games and ice breakers.

9:30 Do activities selected from the Second Sunday of Lent program (pages 16–21).

10:30 Take a break.

11:00 Do activities selected from the Third Sunday of Lent program (pages 22–27).

Saturday Afternoon

12:00 Eat lunch then allow free time.

2:30 Do activities selected from the Fourth Sunday of Lent program (pages 28–33).

3:30 Take a break.

5:00 Do activities selected from the Fifth Sunday of Lent program (pages 34–39).

6:00 Eat dinner.

Saturday Evening

7:00 Do activities and rituals selected from the Maundy Thursday program (pages 46–47). Include an agape feast and/or a foot-washing ritual. (See Worship Ideas on pages 68–69 for more information.)

7:45 Take a break.

8:30 Do activities selected from the Palm Sunday program (pages 40–45).

9:30 Do activities and rituals selected from the Good Friday program (pages 48–49).

10:15 Play games, sing songs, or allow for free time before lights out.

Sunday Morning

8:00 Begin the morning with a sunrise worship service. Incorporate ideas from the Worship Ideas (pages 68–69).

9:00 Eat breakfast.

10:00 Do activities selected from the Easter Sunday program (pages 50–55).

11:00 Clean up and depart.

Additional Resources for Lent

Games for Programs or Retreats

Cardversations™: 104 Questions for Youth to Deal With, by various writers. This discussion-starter kit includes two decks of cards, each card featuring a question to spark discussion, and a leader's guide. Some of these cards deal with Lenten topics such as temptation and sacrifice. Abingdon Press, 2004; ISBN 0-687-74012-6.

Service Projects and Outings

"Youth Ministry, Mission Ideas," from the General Board of Discipleship of The United Methodist Church (*http://www.gbod.org/youth/articles.asp?item_id=8708*). This website lists mission and service opportunities throughout the United States and around the world. Opportunities range from day or weekend projects to week-long trips that could take place during spring break.

Destination Unknown, by Sam Halverson. *Destination Unknown* provides ideas and instructions for fifty mystery trips, some of which relate to the themes and Scriptures used in MISSION: EASTER's programs. Abingdon Press, 2001; ISBN 0-687-0972-4.

Worship Resources

Worship Feast Services: 50 Complete Multisensory Services for Youth, by various writers. *Worship Feast Services* provides orders of service to fit a variety of settings and times of the year, including Lent. Abingdon Press, 2003; ISBN 0-687-06367-1.

Worship Feast Taizé: 20 Complete Services in the Spirit of Taizé, by Jenny Youngman. Taizé-style worship services give the participants a chance to stop and listen to God through meditation and repeatedly singing simple melodies. This worship involves creating a sacred space with crosses, images, and candles and is perfect for the Lenten season. The book includes a music CD. Abingdon Press, 2004; ISBN 0-687-74191-2.

Worship Feast Taizé Songbook: Songs From the Taizé Community provides lyrics, vocal melodies, and guitar chords for popular, easy-to-sing songs from the Taizé community. Abingdon Press, 2004; ISBN 0-687-73932-2.

Bible Studies

3V Bible Studies

- *Radical Jesus,* by Dennis Meaker, looks at Jesus as a man who defied convention and expectations. Abingdon Press, 2003; ISBN 0-687-06528-3.

- *Jesus, the Christ,* by I. Brent Driggers, examines Jesus Christ's divine, saving nature. Abingdon Press, 2003; ISBN 0-687-06538-0.

- *Following Jesus,* by Robin H. Kimbrough, explores what being a disciple of Jesus Christ means. Abingdon Press, 2004; ISBN 0-687-06548-8.

- *Extraordinary New Testament People,* by various writers, tells stories of ordinary people turned extraordinary after encountering Jesus Christ. Abingdon Press, 2004; ISBN 0-687-06558-5.

Bible Dictionary

Bethany: a village about two miles east of Jerusalem that is home to Jesus' friends Mary and Martha in Luke and to their brother Lazarus in John. Bethany is the location of the present-day West Bank village El-Azarieh (an Arabic form of Lazarus' name) and should not be confused with "Bethany across the Jordan," where John performed baptisms (John 1:28).

Canaan: the promised land. Canaan is the ancient name of a land in parts of present-day Israel (including the occupied territories) and Lebanon. Canaan was divided into several small city-states, and its precise boundaries are unknown.

Canaan shares a name with the grandson of Noah introduced in Genesis 9:18. When Ham sees his father Noah lying naked and informs his brothers, Shem and Japheth, Ham's son Canaan is cursed. Noah says, "Cursed be Canaan; lowest of slaves shall he be to his brothers" (Genesis 9:25).

Many Israelite prophets and leaders did not care for Canaanite culture or religion. The Canaanites worshiped gods associated with nature, such as Baal, the rain God. The ancient Israelites considered themselves descendants of Shem and Canaanites descendants of Canaan. Because of the curse on Canaan, some Israelites felt that the Canaanites were destined to be their slaves.

Crucifixion: a form of public execution that was used in the ancient Roman world. Crucifixion was reserved for violent criminals from low classes and for people considered a political threat. The Romans would tie or nail the victim to a cross, which consisted of a large stake and a crossbeam. Death by crucifixion often took days and was the combined result of suffocation, hunger, exposure, and other factors including the beatings that were often given to prisoners prior to crucifixion.

Denarius: a silver Roman coin. One denarius was worth approximately one day's wages.

Fig Tree: a fruit tree that people have cultivated in the Near East since ancient times. The fig tree produces a sweet, pear-shaped fruit that is eaten fresh or dried into cakes. Fig trees have also remained popular both for their beauty and for providing abundant shade.

Galilee: a region of northern Palestine that was home to Jesus and most of his closest followers. Galilee became a part of the Roman Empire in 63 B.C. From 40 to 4 B.C. Galilee was under the control of Herod the Great. After Herod's death, Herod Antipas, Herod the Great's son, governed Galilee. The region's major cities were Sepphoris (located just miles from Nazareth) and Tiberias (located on the Sea of Galilee).

We know that Jesus grew up in the Galilean town of Nazareth, began his ministry in Capernaum (a city located on the northern shore of the Sea of Galilee), and spent most of his career in Galilee.

Haran: a city in northern Mesopotamia, located in present-day southeastern Turkey. While Haran would become a city of importance during the period of Assyrian dominance (the late second and early first millenniums B.C.), it figured prominently into the story of the much earlier biblical patriarchs.

The city Haran shares a name with Abram's brother (Lot's father). Some of Abram's other relatives shared names with cities in the same region (for example Terah, Nahor, and Peleg). After Abram had become Abraham, this man would find a wife for his son Isaac in the region of Haran.

Haran was also important to Isaac's son Jacob. After Jacob cheated his brother out of his birthright, his mother, Rebecca, urged him to seek refuge in Haran. There, Jacob would marry his wives and father his children.

Ancient near-eastern pagan religions considered Haran the home of the moon god, Sin.

Jewish Burial: Unlike the ancient Greeks and Romans, who preferred cremation, the Jews customarily buried their dead. Preparing a body for burial involved binding the mouth shut (John 11:44), washing the body (Acts 9:37), anointing it with fragrant oils (Mark 16:1), and wrapping it in cloth such as linen (John 11:44).

Judas Iscariot: one of the twelve disciples who is best known for betraying Jesus. According to John's Gospel, Judas Iscariot is Jesus' treasurer (John 13:9) but is also a thief who steals from the common purse (John 12:4-6). Judas's greed eventually leads him to betray his teacher and leader. (See, for example, Matthew 26:14-16.) In both Matthew and John, Judas's selfishness is in contrast to the selfless devotion of the woman who anoints Jesus. (See Matthew 26:6-13 and John 12:1-8. John identifies the woman as Mary of Bethany.)

All four Gospel writers record Judas's betrayal (Matthew 26:14-16; Mark 14:10-11; Luke 22:3-6; John 18:2-3). And in all four Gospels, Jesus is aware that he has been, or will be, betrayed (Matthew 26:20-25; Mark 14:18-21; Luke 22:21-23; John 13:21-30). The three Synoptic Gospels (Matthew, Mark, and Luke) all mention that Judas receives money for betraying his teacher and leader. Matthew says that when Judas sees that Jesus has been condemned Judas repents and throws down the pieces of silver he has been paid. As his final remorseful act, Judas commits suicide. Matthew says that he hanged himself (Matthew

27:3-5). In Acts, Luke writes that "falling headlong, [Judas] burst open in the middle and all his bowels gushed out" (Acts 1:18b).

Judas was a common name in the first-century Jewish world. Luke and John identify a second of the twelve disciples named Judas (Luke 6:16 and John 14:22), and Mark mentions that one of Jesus' brothers is named Judas (Mark 6:3). Scholars, however, still debate the meaning and significance of the name Iscariot and have suggested three main possibilities: 1) *Ish-Karioth: Ish* is Hebrew for "man," so *Ish-Karioth* (which may have been translated Iscariot) would mean "Man of Karioth." If Judas had come from Karioth, a town in Judea, he would have been the only one of the twelve disciples to have come from Judea rather than Galilee. 2) *Sicarii:* The Sicarii were a group of radical Jewish assassins, to which Judas may have belonged; Iscariot may have been derived from Sicarii. 3) *Issachar:* Judas may have traced his lineage to the Israelite tribe of Issachar, as Iscariot is similar to Issachar.

Lazarus: Mary and Martha's brother, whom Jesus raises from the dead in John's Gospel. The story of Lazarus's death and resurrection is arguably the climax of the Gospel of John. Where the Synoptic Gospels (Matthew, Mark, and Luke) tell of miracles, John tells of signs. A miracle in Mark, for example, is an extraordinary deed that Jesus performs for the health or restoration of another person (and sometimes performs in secret). A sign in John, on the other hand, is an extraordinary deed Jesus performs so that all who witness this sign will believe that Jesus is God's Son. Raising Lazarus from the dead is Jesus' final and most impressive sign. This sign also inspires some Pharisees and chief priests to launch a plot to kill Jesus (John 11:45-53). Because Lazarus's resurrection so angers Jesus' critics, some chief priests plot to kill Lazarus as well (12:9-11).

Compare the raising from the dead of Jairus's daughter (Mark 5:21-24, 35-43) with the Lazarus story in John. Jesus goes to Jairus's daughter soon after learning of her death, but Lazarus lay dead for four days before Jesus' arrival. Prior to Lazarus' death, messengers from Mary and

© 2005 Abingdon Press. Permission is granted to reproduce this page for use with MISSION: EASTER—YOUTH PROGRAMS & IDEAS FOR LENT. All rights reserved.

Martha inform Jesus that their brother is ill. Jesus tells the messengers that the illness is "for God's glory" (John 11:4) and waits two days before journeying to Lazarus' home in Bethany. After raising Jairus's daughter, Jesus instructs witnesses to tell no one (Mark 5:43). By contrast, Jesus' raising of Lazarus is performed in front of a crowd "so that they may believe" (John 11:38-42). The differences between these two stories may be explained by when in the course of Jesus' ministry they take place. Jairus's daughter is raised from the dead relatively early in Jesus' career, while Lazarus's return to life occurs in the weeks leading up to Jesus' death.

The Gospel of John suggests that Lazarus is one of Jesus' closest friends. Mary and Martha's message to Jesus reads, "Lord, he whom you love is ill" (John 11:3b). When discussing Lazarus' death with his disciples, Jesus refers to "our friend Lazarus" (11:11); and upon arriving at Lazarus's tomb, Jesus famously weeps (11:35).

Lazarus, as a person and friend of Jesus, does not appear in Matthew, Mark, or Luke. But Jesus uses a character named Lazarus in his parable of the rich man and Lazarus (Luke 16:19-31). All Jesus says about the character Lazarus is that he is poor, hungry, homeless, and "covered with sores" (Luke 16:20) and that when he dies he is carried away to heaven (Luke 16:22). When the rich man who ignores Lazarus dies, he goes to Hades where he is tormented; "a great chasm has been fixed" between him and Lazarus (Luke 16:26a). No clear connection, however, is known between Lazarus the friend of Jesus and Lazarus the character in the parable.

Mary of Bethany: a woman whom in separate accounts in Luke and John Jesus praises when she acts in a way that others find objectionable. In Luke 10:38-42, Mary sits at Jesus' feet, listening to what he has to say, while her sister, Martha, is left to perform household tasks alone. Martha asks Jesus, "Lord do you not care that my sister has left me to do all the work by myself?" (Luke 10:40).

In John 12:1-8 Mary "took a pound of costly perfume made of pure nard, anointed Jesus' feet, and wiped them with her hair" (John 12:3). In the context of John's Gospel, Mary symbolically anoints Jesus for burial. Judas Iscariot protests because the expensive oil could be sold to assist the poor. (The text adds that Judas wasn't truly concerned for the poor but was looking for money to steal from the treasury.)

In both cases, Jesus sides with Mary and holds her up as a truly devoted disciple. Both accounts present Mary as someone who is not burdened by anxiety or how she might be perceived. She is contrasted by Martha, who is anxious about getting her work done, and Judas, who is anxious about money.

Mary Magdalene: a woman prominent among Jesus' disciples. In every list of Jesus' female followers, Mary's name comes first (Matthew 27:55-56, 61; 28:1; Mark 15:40-41, 47; 16:1; Luke 8:2-3; 24:10). All four Gospels mention Mary among the women who came to Jesus' tomb on the morning after the sabbath and to whom Jesus first appeared following his resurrection. Luke also tells us that Mary was one of the women who provided for Jesus' ministry "out of their resources" (Luke 8:2-3).

Tradition has labeled Mary Magdalene a prostitute, though Scripture says nothing of Mary's occupation. Luke mentions that "seven demons had gone out" of Mary (Luke 8:2), and some people have concluded that Mary had been living an immoral life (such as a life of prostitution) before Jesus healed her.

Some traditions have also suggested that Mary was Jesus' wife. (This theory has been popularized recently by the success of Dan Brown's novel *The DaVinci Code*.) Though we can assume that Jesus and Mary were close, Scripture in no way suggests that they were married. The Gospel of Philip, which is not found in the Bible, suggests that Jesus' male disciples

were jealous of their teacher's close relationship with Mary. Because no complete version of The Gospel of Philip exists, we do not know the details of this relationship. At any rate, most scholars agree that The Gospel of Philip was written much later than the biblical Gospels and is not historically reliable, though it may reflect some early Christian traditions.

Mary's name suggests that she is from Magdala, a fishing village on the western shore of the Sea of Galilee. Like Jesus and the Twelve disciples (except, possibly, Judas Iscariot), Mary was Galilean.

Martha: a female disciple of Jesus who, unlike her sister Mary, is easily distracted by the demands of running a household. Luke introduces Martha in 10:38b as a woman who "welcomed [Jesus] into her home." That she invites Jesus into her house suggests she is the head of her household. John tells us in 11:5, "Jesus loved Martha and her sister and Lazarus." John emphasizes Martha's importance as a disciple by listing her first. John also records a conversation between Martha and Jesus when Jesus arrives in Bethany following the death of Lazarus, Martha's brother. Their conversation concludes with Martha confessing, "Yes, Lord, I believe that you are the Messiah, the Son of God, the one coming into the world" (John 11:27).

However, Luke and John both suggest that Martha's relationship with Jesus is not as intimate as her sister's. In Luke 10:40, Martha is "distracted by her many tasks" while Mary sits at Jesus' feet. In John 12:2-3, Martha serves dinner to Jesus and other guests while Mary anoints Jesus' feet with expensive ointment and wipes his feet with her hair.

Parable: a short story that uses a metaphor to teach a lesson. Parables press the listener to determine to what or to whom the parable refers. The listener must also figure out what the parable is saying about its subject.

Jesus' parables are prominent in all three Synoptic Gospels (Matthew, Mark, and Luke), especially Luke. Well-known parables such as those about the good Samaritan, the rich man and Lazarus, and the prodigal son are unique to Luke's Gospel. The extrabiblical Gospel of Thomas, discovered in Egypt in 1945 and thought by some scholars to include accurate sayings of Jesus, includes some parables found in the biblical Gospels (such as the parables of the wicked tenants, the lost sheep, and the rich fool) as well as some parables that are unique to Thomas.

Parables can also be found in the Old Testament. In fact, Jesus' parable of the wicked tenants (Matthew 21:33-42; Mark 12:1-11; Luke 20:9-18) is modeled after Isaiah's song about the unfruitful vineyard (Isaiah 5:1-2). The prophet Nathan also tells a parable when he confronts David about committing adultery with Bathsheba and having Bathsheba's husband, Uriah, killed (2 Samuel 12:1-4).

Passover: A Jewish religious festival commemorating the "passing over" of Hebrew households during the plague of the firstborn. (See Exodus 12:1–13:16.) The celebration of the festival dates back to the ancient Israelites. (For example, see Joshua 5:10-12 and 2 Kings 23:21-23.) The most important Jewish festival, Passover celebrates freedom and redemption, specifically the liberation from slavery in Egypt. Passover celebrations traditionally center on a feast, or Seder. Current-day Seders are multi-course meals that symbolically retell the Passover story through foods, blessings, and rituals.

The Synoptic Gospels (Matthew, Mark, and Luke) suggest that Jesus' last supper with his disciples was a Passover Seder held on the first day of the Passover festival. In John, however, Jesus shares his final meal on the evening before the beginning of the festival and is crucified on the first day of Passover. (All of the Gospels agree that Jesus dies on a Friday, but John differs on the day Passover begins.) For John Jesus is the ultimate Passover lamb (or paschal

© 2005 Abingdon Press. Permission is granted to reproduce this page for use with
MISSION: EASTER—YOUTH PROGRAMS & IDEAS FOR LENT. All rights reserved.

lamb—see Exodus 12:21-27). Just as the blood of the lambs sacrificed on the first Passover saved Hebrew households from the angel of death, the blood of Jesus saves humankind from death.

Pilate, Pontius: the Roman prefect (high military official acting as governor) in Judea from 26 to 36 A.D. Pilate is best known for his role in Jesus' trial and crucifixion. While Pilate's level of involvement in these events is disputed, only Pilate would have been able to authorize an execution by crucifixion.

Pilate was notorious among first-century Jews for his brutality and for sneaking statues of the emperor, which were considered idolatrous, into Jerusalem. (The statues were removed after massive nonviolent protest.) The famous Jewish historian Flavius Josephus records an incident when the prefect had a Samaritan prophet and his many followers, who were peacefully gathered on Mount Gerizim, slaughtered as insurrectionists. Luke 13:1 speaks of "the Galileans whose blood Pilate had mingled with their sacrifices," which suggests that Pilate also had authorized a massacre somehow related to the Galileans' religious practices.

Sabbath: a day of rest on which work is restricted or prohibited. Recognition of the sabbath was an instrumental part of ancient Israelite religion that was mandated by the Ten Commandments (Exodus 20:8-11). 2 Kings 4:23 suggests that later in Israel's history the sabbath was a regular day to visit the Temple. The prophet Jeremiah also emphasizes the importance and holiness of the sabbath (Jeremiah 17:19-27). According to Old Testament law, failure to observe the sabbath was punishable by death. (See Exodus 31:12-17 and Numbers 15:32-36.)

We know that the sabbath was important to religious life in Jesus' day, because Jesus openly disagreed with religious leaders as to how the sabbath should be observed. Jesus heals on the sabbath (Mark 3:1-5; Luke 13:10-17; and John 5:1-18), and his disciples pluck heads of grain on the day of rest (Matthew 12:1-8 and Mark 2:23-27). Certain religious leaders condemn these actions, but Jesus wittingly answers his critics

with statements such as, "The sabbath was made for humankind, and not humankind for the sabbath" (Mark 2:27); "Is it lawful to do good or to do harm on the sabbath, to save life or to kill?" (Mark 3:4); and "The Son of Man is lord of the sabbath" (Matthew 12:8).

Siloam, Tower of: a tower that was probably part of the old Jerusalem city walls that rose above the pool of Siloam. The pool of Siloam was a reservoir located on the south side of the old city of Jerusalem. The pool was connected to the spring of Gihon, Jerusalem's principle water source, by a tunnel, providing a water source within the city walls.

In Luke 13:4 Jesus mentions "eighteen who were killed when the tower of Siloam fell on them" and adds that these people were no "worse offenders than all the others living in Jerusalem." That is, tragedy is not linked to sinfulness. Rather, all are sinful and all should repent.

Simon the Cyrene: the man said to have carried Jesus' cross (Matthew 27:32; Mark 15:21; Luke 23:26). While Jesus would have carried the crossbeam (John 19:17), he would not have carried the entire cross. By taking up the cross, Simon literally does what Jesus calls us all to do figuratively. (See Matthew 16:24.)

Cyrene was a city located in what is currently Libya. The city had a large Jewish community in Jesus' time.

Tomb: During Roman times, Jews (like their Hebrew and Israelite predecessors) buried their dead in the ground. While this practice does not seem unusual today, cremation was far more common in the ancient Roman world. Jewish tombs ranged from unmarked holes in the ground to holes marked with stones to alcoves dug into soft, limestone caves.

Jesus was apparently buried in a limestone cave. Like most cavernous tombs,

---

© 2005 Abingdon Press. Permission is granted to reproduce this page for use with
MISSION: EASTER—YOUTH PROGRAMS & IDEAS FOR LENT. All rights reserved.

Jesus' tomb was covered by a large, stone wheel that rolled along a track or groove in the ground. Such tombs were usually available only to the wealthy, but the Gospels suggest that Jesus' tomb was owned by a "righteous man named Joseph" from "the Jewish town of Arimathea" (Luke 23:50-51). Luke mentions that Joseph was also a member of the council that tried Jesus, though Joseph "had not agreed to their plan and action" (Luke 23:50-51).

Trial of Jesus: In Judea, at the time of Jesus' trial and crucifixion, the Roman prefect (high military official acting as governor), Pontius Pilate, had the ultimate authority in matters of law and justice. The Gospels suggest that religious leaders brought Jesus to trial, but only Pilate could determine Jesus' guilt or innocence and his sentence. In all four Gospel accounts, an angry mob influences Pilate's decision; but Pilate's sentence of crucifixion, a very public form of execution, suggests that he also regarded him as a political threat. (See Matthew 27:11-26; Mark 15:1-15; Luke 23:1-5, 13-25; and John 18:28–19:16.)

All four Gospels include a pre-trial presided over by religious leaders. Matthew, Mark, and Luke mention Jesus' trial before the Sanhedrin, a council of Jewish religious leaders (Matthew 26:57-68; Mark 14:53-65; Luke 22:66-71). In all three cases, Jesus is found guilty of blasphemy because he insists or implies that he is the Son of God. In John 18:19-24, a high priest questions Jesus. While the high priest does not accuse Jesus of blasphemy, he is apparently upset by Jesus' boldness.

Only Luke tells of Jesus' trial before Herod Antipas, who governed Galilee (Luke 23:6-12). According to Luke, Pilate sends Jesus to Herod upon learning that Jesus is Galilean. Legally, this move was not necessary, though it may have been an act of courtesy. Since Jesus was accused and arrested in Judea, the Roman prefect in Judea, Pilate, had the complete authority to try and sentence him.

Wilderness: untamed and uninhabited land. For Jesus, the "wilderness" would have been the dry, rocky deserts and steppes of ancient Palestine. The wilderness in the story of Jesus' temptation is often thought to be the desert land of the Sinai Peninsula. Though the peninsula, located in present-day Egypt, is bounded by the Mediterranean Sea and the Gulfs of Suez and Aqaba (both extensions of the Red Sea), Sinai is quite dry, usually receiving fewer than 2.5 inches of rain per year.

Because life in the desert wilderness was difficult and uncomfortable, some biblical writers considered the land a home of evil spirits. Luke 11:24, for example, speaks of unclean spirits wandering "through the waterless region." Isaiah speaks of the land of Edom being turned into a desolate wilderness where "goat-demons shall call to each other" and where "Lilith [a female demon] shall repose, and find a place to rest" (Isaiah 34:14).

The desert's unforgiving terrain and the idea that such land was home to demons made the wilderness the obvious location for trials and tests. The beloved story of the ancient Hebrews led by Moses includes an extremely trying, forty-year trek through the Sinai wilderness. When Elijah was running from Queen Jezebel, he headed for the wilderness, where he questioned whether he should go on living.

Like his predecessors Moses and Elijah, Jesus was tested in the wilderness. Jesus' wilderness experience, however, went much smoother than those of Moses and Elijah. While Moses once "broke faith" with God (Deuteronomy 32:51) and Elijah once asked God to take his life, Jesus boldly dealt with each challenge he faced. And ultimately, the devil left Jesus, "and suddenly angels came and waited on him" (Matthew 4:11). The story of Jesus' testing is recorded in all three Synoptic Gospels (Matthew, Mark, and Luke), though Mark does not describe the three temptations.

Dictionary entries written by Josh Tinley